T0380721

INSPIRATIONS
Spoken Day By Day

WITH FAITH, HOPE, AND LOVE

DEBRA DOMINO

Featuring Quotes By:
Doris Freeman, Sister Love

BALBOA.PRESS
A DIVISION OF HAY HOUSE

Balboa Press books may be ordered through booksellers or by contacting:

Balboa Press
A Division of Hay House
1663 Liberty Drive
Bloomington, IN 47403
www.balboapress.com
844-682-1282

Because of the dynamic nature of the Internet, any web addresses or
links contained in this book may have changed since publication and
may no longer be valid. The views expressed in this work are solely those
of the author and do not necessarily reflect the views of the publisher,
and the publisher hereby disclaims any responsibility for them.

The author of this book does not dispense medical advice or prescribe the use
of any technique as a form of treatment for physical, emotional, or medical
problems without the advice of a physician, either directly or indirectly. The
intent of the author is only to offer information of a general nature to help
you in your quest for emotional and spiritual well-being. In the event you use
any of the information in this book for yourself, which is your constitutional
right, the author and the publisher assume no responsibility for your actions.

Any people depicted in stock imagery provided by Getty Images are
models, and such images are being used for illustrative purposes only.
Certain stock imagery © Getty Images.

Scripture quotations marked NIV are taken from the Holy Bible, New
International Version®. NIV®. Copyright © 1973, 1978, 1984 by International
Bible Society. Used by permission of Zondervan. All rights reserved. [Biblica]

Print information available on the last page.

ISBN: 978-1-9822-7215-9 (sc)
ISBN: 978-1-9822-7216-6 (e)

Library of Congress Control Number: 2021914849

Balboa Press rev. date: 08/11/2021

CONTENTS

PERSONAL PAGES FOR NOTES

DEDICATION

In Loving Memory of Pastor Jerrel
Dean Coleman. Thank you for showing
me your undying faith and belief.

ACKNOWLEDGEMENTS

Debra Domino, Author *Reflections of Omnipotent Love and Open Your Greatest Gift*

Thank you so much Rowena Brown Trent and Doris Freeman for inspiring me to take the journey to compose INSPIRATIONS SPOKEN DAY BY DAY – WITH FAITH, HOPE, AND LOVE. Sometimes, the most peaceful sanctuary is the dome of the mind and what is visualized and heard by the ears on each side of the dome. Inspirational thoughts can be calming for the soul. This vision was created during a time of crisis when I needed it the most.

Rowena Brown Trent, thank you very much for your undying faith and friendship. You saw the need for the uplift and you ingeniously started a daily text to check in to make sure to say something kind and uplifting to start the day. That act of compassion is what jumpstarted my day. It gave me the hope to keep going and the love to see me through. It is just that simple to tap into something so very powerful that it has the power to light up the world. I looked forward to hearing my phone beep each day to see what your message would say and how it would create thoughts to inspire me for the day and sometimes the rest of the week. That act of faith inspired the name "Sister Faith"; and your strong belief felt like it had the power to move mountains. You unselfishly gave a gift to step in as another sister after the loss of my beloved sisters, Versia Mae and Lucy Mae. Thank you very much "Sister Faith."

Doris Freeman, my biological sister – thank you so much for joining right in and speaking loving messages from the heart. You were adorned with the name "Sister Love." Your spirit has always brought the loving actions and endearment to our family. I love the way you would chime in with your thoughts each morning after Rowena sent the initial text to check in for the day. It amazed me how you found the right words to put the icing on the cake as a figure of speech. You are lovingly such a good baker of homemade pound cakes and amazingly you found a way to bring that art to the spirit of inspiration with your endearing words each day. Thank you my "Sister Love."

It was such an enlightening spiritual exercise to take part in with you ladies each day. I, Debra Domino, chimed in with the name "Sister Hope." You two ladies gave me so much hope, and love that my faith was enthused in such a brilliant way. The three virtues of Faith, Hope, and Love were infused to make something so special for our relationship. It gives me much pleasure to introduce this book of daily inspirations day by day that can be referenced each day of the year for many years to come. ***INSPIRATIONS SPOKEN DAY BY DAY - WITH FAITH, HOPE, AND LOVE*** helped me to navigate the offerings of the bible in an old fashioned way similar to what I studied as a child in Sunday school, but with a modern day type of twist of the lens of the microscope and concurring along with day to day events happening in the world. It gives me great pleasure to present this book inspired by the faithful actions of Rowena Brown Trent, Sister Faith and featuring loving quotes of Love by Doris Freeman, Sister Love. Thank you both ladies for opening your gifts up for me.

I would be remiss if I did not also honorably mention the inspirations of my life posthumously. Versia Mae Williams McCauley Moore, my oldest sister – If you were here alive in spirit to take part in this project, your name would be "Sister Patience." Your strength for Patience and Perseverance was so remarkable during your faithful and loving journey on this earth. Lucy Mae Williams, my second oldest sister – If you were here alive in spirit to take part in this project, your name would be "Sister Peace." You were always the peace-maker in every situation even when it appeared that Peace was not deserved. Thank you for the Peace and love that you gave unconditionally for your family.

Love,
Debra Domino

INSPIRATIONS

Rowena Brown Trent
"Sister Faith"

Ephesians 2:8 "For it is by grace you have been saved, through faith -and this is not from yourselves, it is the gift of God"

I heard that the things that most impact our lives are the books we read and the people we meet. This statement certainly applies to my friend Debra Domino (Sister Hope) and her latest inspirational book.

She certainly has impacted my life through reading this book. The book is full of bible scriptures, and beautiful quotes from Debra Domino (Sister Hope) and Doris Freeman (Sister Love). This book is very uplifting and encouraging. If you're looking for inspiration it's all in this must-read book.

Debra, I am honored to be part of this awesome inspirational project. Please continue to Grace us with your books of unity that started with faith, love, and hope. I have faith that this book is going to impact and save many lives.

Faithfully Yours,
Rowena Brown Trent (Sister Faith)

INSPIRATIONS

**Doris Freeman,
"Sister Love"**

Corinthians 13:13 "And now these three remain: faith, hope, and love; but the greatest of these is love."

When Debra first mentioned putting our quotes on a daily calendar to be made into a book for 366 days of the year, which includes the years with a leap day. I became so excited. I wanted the world to have something that they can look at any current date of the month and get something out of our messages to inspire them to have a better day.

I enjoy giving love and making people feel loved, which I am hoping that the positive vibes from these messages will help them make decisions that will create love, peace, and make them happy.

Debra Domino is a big inspiration to me, because of the passion and tenacity that motivates her to write. I want to thank her for allowing me to be a part of this book, and for being my role model as an Author and my sister.

I love you Sis.

Doris Freeman (Sister Love)

INTRODUCTION

Coming together in the spirit of Faith, Hope, and Love three sisters dedicated each day to sincere heartfelt communications between each other as a daily ritual to stimulate and uplift the emotions to empower the fortitude needed to begin each day. The daily connection became like a type of therapy for the soul that inspired other thoughts and ideas needed to handle the encounters of daily life and its situations. This conception coined the names for each sister Faith, Hope, and Love. Faith brought the strong belief and dedication to the power of remaining steadfast in what may not be seen is always there to guide the way. Hope brought the courage and confidence that faith had laid the foundation for something great to come with the optimism and anticipation that each new day of life could deliver the needed bounty. Love brought the compassion, devotion, and caring space to hold the visions of faith, and hope in a shelter filled with all the necessary ingredients to uplift, unify, and empower with secure and loving arms.

This daily connection formed layers of support to mentally sustain and physically walk in faith, hope, and loving harmony each day. There may be many other trios who are doing or desire to do this daily practice of alignment. This book is dedicated to the sharing of this purpose to be used to empower your day. Love is like a flower forever blooming. Faith is the bedrock of your inner-self. It is like the jewel of birth holding the belief. Hope is the promise, trust, and aspiration that dreams and goals will be fulfilled.

JANUARY 1

HAPPY NEW YEAR!

Exodus 12:2 "This month shall be unto
you the beginning of months: it shall be
the first month of the year to you."

Step forward and begin the year of new
Know in your heart that all is with you
Seek the love that you want to find
Know that it starts with simply being kind

Contributed By: Debra Domino

JANUARY 2

Jeremiah 29:11-13 [11]"For I know the plans I have for you," declares the Lord, "plans to prosper you and not to harm you, plans to give you hope and a future. [12]Then you will call on me and come and pray to me, and I will listen to you. [13]You will seek me and find me when you seek me with all your heart."

What a blessing to see the first month of the year
Another year has passed with open paths to clear
See, seek, make plans, move forward and pray
Know within your heart that God will lead the way

Contributed By: Debra Domino

Hosea 6:2 "After two days he will revive
us; on the third day he will restore us,
that we may live in his presence."

Rise Up, Renew, Restore and Rejoice
Another day has come to stake claim with your voice
Make the changes that you want to see
You have control over whatever you want to be

Contributed By: Debra Domino

JANUARY 4

Psalm 91:10 "If you say, "The LORD is my refuge," and you make the Most High your dwelling, [10]- no harm will overtake you, no disaster will come near your tent."

Remember the shelter in the time of storm
It may seem odd when presented in another form
Your dwelling of protection your home your hood
Just know that it's all working for the greater good

Contributed By: Debra Domino

JANUARY 5

Psalm 37:5-6 "Commit your way to the LORD; trust in him and he will do this: [6]He will make your righteous reward shine like the dawn, your vindication like the noonday sun."

Commit to your duty of works at dawn

Step forward in action in the noonday sun

Trust in the word and let your light shine bright

The reward in knowing that wrongs will be made right

Contributed By: Debra Domino

JANUARY 6

Matthew 5:14–16 "You are the light of the world.
A city that is set on a hill cannot be hidden.
¹⁵"Nor do they light a lamp and put it under a
basket, but on a lampstand, and it gives light to
all [who are] in the house. ¹⁶"Let your light so
shine before men, that they may see your good
works and glorify your Father in heaven."

Receive the power grid always running and lighting
Giving the favor needed so no need for the fighting
For thousands of generations shining and confessing
That the eternal power grid is the light and the blessing

Contributed By: Debra Domino

JANUARY 7

Romans 8:28 "And we know that for those who love God all things work together for good, for those who are called according to his purpose."

Work together for the common good of all
Rise up with great purpose and stand tall
Believe in your worth with great anticipation
Fulfilling the purpose with strong determination

Contributed By: Debra Domino

Proverbs 15:30 "A cheerful look brings joy to the heart; good news makes for good health."

Smile with grace from ear to ear

The look of joy spreads good cheer

Good news and good health yield the fresh start

The wealth of health is good for the heart

Contributed By: Debra Domino

JANUARY 9

Colossians 3:17 "And whatever you do, whether in word or deed, do it all in the name of the LORD Jesus, giving thanks to God the Father through him."

Many may walk in the duty of their works
Critical issues may darken the perks
Deeds of compassion in the line of action
The reward is appreciation with God's satisfaction

Contributed By: Debra Domino

JANUARY 10

Ephesians 4:31 "Get rid of all bitterness, rage and anger, brawling and slander, along with every form of malice."

The bitterness of rage and anger challenge defeat
The bitter roots sprout trouble for history to repeat
Overturn the malice from bitter to sweet
Restoring grace and honor for the soul's retreat

Contributed By: Debra Domino

JANUARY 11

Corinthians 10:13 "There hath no temptation taken
you but such as is common to man: but God is faithful,
who will not suffer you to be tempted above that
ye are able; but will with the temptation also make
a way to escape, that ye may be able to bear it."

Coercion may come presenting temptations
Stay true to your faith to see the revelations
The plan will unfold to expose what is true
Your will gives the power to see you through

Contributed By: Debra Domino

JANUARY 12

Proverbs 13:12 "Hope deferred makes the heart sick, but a longing fulfilled is a tree of life."

Hope deferred can make the heart feel deprived

A vision of hope keeps the spirit alive

Grounded in faith gives the endurance

The tree of life brings fulfillment and assurance

Contributed By: Debra Domino

JANUARY 13

Deuteronomy 31:6 "Be strong and courageous.
Do not be afraid or terrified because of them,
for the LORD your God goes with you; he
will never leave you nor forsake you."

Strength building for the courage to face the fear inside

Anxiety of the emotions can make the feelings terrified

Deep inside your gut the valor may start to rumble

The gallantry of the spirit to make the fear crumble

Contributed By: Debra Domino

JANUARY 14

Ephesians 6:10 "Finally, be strong in the
LORD and in his mighty power."

Feel the strength of your power and let it roar

Set your intentions and let your energy soar

Your mighty dominion to call on every hour

It's your coat of armor the shield of your power

Contributed By: Debra Domino

JANUARY 15

Jeremiah 23:16. "They speak visions from their own minds, not from the mouth of the LORD."

WITH FAITH, HOPE, AND LOVE
the vision of your aspiration

From your mind to your heart with
breaths of anticipation

The visualization of what is seen is believed

The realization of your dreams and the goals achieved

Contributed By: Debra Domino

JANUARY 16

Acts 20:35 "In everything, I showed you that by this kind of hard work we must help the weak, remembering the words of the Lord Jesus Himself: **'It is more blessed to give than to receive."**

Works of service are civil acts of giving

Helping others is a universal part of living

Giving of your essence in the time of need

Can return blessings for you to succeed

Contributed By: Debra Domino

JANUARY 17

Matthew 18:15 "If your brother or sister sins, go and point out their fault, just between the two of you. If they listen to you, you have won them over."

Much can be learned from a reprimand

Communication and caring go hand in hand

Listening is the key to comprehending

For better or for worse is not about pretending

Contributed By: Debra Domino

JANUARY 18

Psalm 35:10 "Every fiber of my being will
shout, "Eternal One, there is none like You!
You save the poor. from those who try to
overpower them. and rescue the weak and the
needy from those who steal from them."

Every fiber of your being has power in each cell
Working and moving constantly trying to keep you well
Like mini soldiers on guard for your protection
Restoring and replenishing for daily resurrection

Contributed By: Debra Domino

JANUARY 19

Psalm 107:19 "Then they cried to the LORD in their trouble, and he saved them from their distress."

Some days may seem filled with distress
The harder you work the more the duress
Take a humble time out to and cry out
For help and strength to handle the bout

Contributed By: Debra Domino

JANUARY 20

Corinthians 5:9 "So whether we are at home or away, we make it our aim to please him."

Priority for yourself is an important goal
The key to self-worth is what you hold
Aim to be pleasing in your own sight
The vision emitted shines your own light

Contributed By: Debra Domino

JANUARY 21

Corinthians 16:20 "All the brothers and sisters here send you greetings. Greet one another with a holy kiss."

A hug is a gesture to embrace and enfold
A sincere expression that never grows old
The greeting of one another whether kiss or no kiss
The spirit of your intention dwells in the midst

Contributed By: Debra Domino

JANUARY 22

Psalm 42:8 "By day the Lord directs his love, at night his song is with me— a prayer to the God of my life."

A new day of rising is filled with God's love
Songs from the night birds chirping above
The existence of life and its blessings to behold
The future to unfold and the stories to be told

Contributed By: Debra Domino

JANUARY 23

Habakkuk 2:2 "And the LORD answered me,
and said, Write the vision, and make it plain
upon tables, that he may run that readeth it."

Upon tablets, tables, scripts to be read
The handwriting of your mind speaks to be said
The vision in view written plain and clear
For the world to see and the minds to hear

Contributed By: Debra Domino

JANUARY 24

Thessalonians 5:11 "Therefore encourage one another and build each other up, just as in fact you are doing."

Today is one for complimenting one another
Like the help and encouragement given by a mother
The support and motivation can also stimulate
Inspiration and ideas to help you create

Contributed By: Debra Domino

JANUARY 25

John 16:33 "I have told you these things, so that in me you may have peace. In this world you will have trouble. But take heart! I have overcome the world."

Opposition to peace can feel like cruel domination

Pain inflicted by others invokes the plea for liberation

But why the persecution and not God's affection

Trouble comes and goes but there's
always God's protection

Contributed By: Debra Domino

JANUARY 26

Ecclesiastes 4:9 "Two are better than one, because
they have a good return for their labor"

A day to celebrate the union of partnership
The power of two strengthens the relationship
The alliance together can be robust and fun
The results of the labor can produce a great return

Contributed By: Debra Domino

JANUARY 27

Acts 7:22 "And Moses was learned in all the wisdom of the Egyptians, and was mighty in words and in deeds."

Education and learning make for wisdom with insight
The works of these principles can bring much might
Words turned to deeds can help restore
A nation in recovery will upturn with much more

Contributed By: Debra Domino

JANUARY 28

Proverbs 27:9 "Oil and perfume make the
heart glad, and the sweetness of a friend
comes from his earnest counsel".

The sweetness of a friend makes gladness for the heart

Like sweet perfume with an aroma that never parts

A ring of honor with earnest class

A true friendship is one that will last

Contributed By: Debra Domino

JANUARY 29

Genesis 15:5 "He took him outside and said,
"Look up at the sky and count the stars–if
indeed you can count them." Then he said
to him, "So shall your offspring be."

Gazing upon the glory of the stars in the sky
The mystery of how many and the reason why
Believing that you can count them and also shine
Gives the answer to the conundrum for all mankind

Contributed By: Debra Domino

JANUARY 30

Romans 12:17 "Do not repay anyone evil for evil. Be careful to do what is right in the eyes of everyone."

Evil lurks around in all places
It comes in many forms and has many faces
Be careful when challenged in plain sight
Be the better person and do what's right

Contributed By: Debra Domino

JANUARY 31

Exodus 35:35 "He has filled them with skill to do all kinds of work as engravers, designers, embroiderers in blue, purple and scarlet yarn and fine linen, and weavers-all of them skilled workers and designers."

The skills to do many different works of art
To build and design right from the heart
The wisdom to create from God's gift to your hand
The masterwork of sculptures throughout the land

Contributed By: Debra Domino

FEBRUARY 1

Luke 10:27 "So he answered and said, "You shall love the Lord your God with all your heart, with all your soul, with all your soul, with all your strength, and with all your mind, and your neighbor as yourself."

The circle of Life completes your
circle of love. Give love daily.

Quoted By: Doris Freeman (Sister Love)

FEBRUARY 2

Ecclesiastes 1:5 - "The sun rises and the sun
sets; it hurries back to where it rises."

**Whether it will be the shadow with sunshine
or the dark shadows of clouds, to weather
the weather of the seasons of winter or
early spring; keep healthy minds and clean
souls to acquire love and prosperity.**

Quoted By: Doris Freeman (Sister Love)

FEBRUARY 3

Psalms 30:5 "For his anger last only a moment, but his favor lasts a lifetime; weeping stay for the night, but rejoicing comes in the morning."

Morning is a creator of the first day of the rest of our life, an energy booster.

Quoted By: Doris Freeman (Sister Love)

FEBRUARY 4

Job 33:4 "The spirit of God has made me, the breath of the Almighty gives me life."

May the breathing of fresh air today be healing to the soul, and provide unlimited wealth, health, and prosperity as it is the gift of life.

Quoted By: Doris Freeman (Sister Love)

FEBRUARY 5

Genesis 13:17 "Arise, walk around the land through the length and breadth, for I will give it to you." You shall teach them diligently to your sons, and shall talk of them when you sit your house and when you walk by the way and when you lie down and when you rise up."

Walk around and savor in the sweetness of the smell, the touch of love and the ripple of breath to see the glory and grace in the light of protection on this beautiful day.

Quoted By: Doris Freeman (Sister Love)

FEBRUARY 6

Proverbs: 10:28-30 "The hope of the righteous brings joy, but the expectation of the wicked will perish. But the fruit of the Spirit is love, joy, peace, patience, kindness, goodness, faithfulness, gentleness, self-control, against such things, there is no law."

Release and exhale the darkness, so that the brightness of joy can be received.

Quoted By: Doris Freeman (Sister Love)

FEBRUARY 7

Proverbs 3: 5-6 "Trust in the Lord with all your heart and do not lean on your own understanding. In all your ways acknowledge him, and he will make straight your paths."

Trusting and receiving the joy may seal the faith with a stake in the victory and power of glory.

Quoted By: Doris Freeman (Sister Love)

FEBRUARY 8

Matthew 10: 16 "Behold I send you out as
sheep in the mist of wolves. Therefore, be
wise as serpents and harmless as doves."

When the storm of life is raging, hold still,
stay steady, until the calm flows through.

Quoted By: Doris Freeman (Sister Love)

FEBRUARY 9

Genesis 9:13 "I have set my rainbow in the clouds, and it will be the sign of the covenant between me and the earth."

Do not be afraid to walk through the rain to get to the rainbow.

Quoted By: Doris Freeman (Sister Love)

FEBRUARY 10

Corinthians 5:17 "Therefore, if anyone is in Christ, he is a new creation. The old has passed away, behold, the new has come."

Each day we begin a new paragraph of life for the chapter that we are currently in. You have the ability to change the story as we go. Make it fun and happy.

Quoted By: Doris Freeman (Sister Love)

FEBRUARY 11

Proverbs 29:11 "A fool gives full vent to his
spirit, but a wise man quietly holds it back."

Each person is made of a kaleidoscope of emotions,
that they shall conquer in their own special way.

Quoted By: Doris Freeman (Sister Love)

FEBRUARY 12

Romans 12:10 "Love one another with brotherly affection. Outdo one another in showing honor."

Give love abundantly, and you will
receive an abundance of joy.

Quoted By: Doris Freeman (Sister Love)

FEBRUARY 13

Psalm 16:11 "You make known to me the path of life; in your presence there is fullness of joy, at your right hand are pleasures forevermore."

Make somebody smile today.

Quoted By: Doris Freeman (Sister Love)

FEBRUARY 14

Valentines Day: A Day for Love.

Galatians 5:22 "But the fruit of the Spirit is love, joy, peace, patience, kindness, goodness and faithfulness."

Love is in the air swirling everywhere. Shower your love one, today, with love, gifts, and surprises.

Quoted By: Doris Freeman (Sister Love)

FEBRUARY 15

Job: 6:6 NIV "Is tasteless food eaten without salt, or is there flavor in the sap of the mallow?"

Enjoy the flavor of life while we can still taste it.

Quoted By: Doris Freeman (Sister Love)

FEBRUARY 16

Ecclesiastes 3:11 "He has made everything
beautiful in its time. He has also set eternity in
the human heart, yet no one can fathom what
God has done from beginning to end."

Life is amazing when we see the beauty,
instead of taking it for granted. Savor
the sweetness of the blessings.

Quoted By: Doris Freeman (Sister Love)

FEBRUARY 17

Matthew 13:31 "The Kingdom of heaven is like a mustard seed, which a man took and sowed in his field."

When you step out on faith and believe, that Mustard Seed expands to a size without limitations.

Quoted By: Doris Freeman (Sister Love)

FEBRUARY 18

Corinthians 5:17 "The same God who takes
a caterpillar and changes it into a butterfly,
transforms sinners into saints."

You may start out as a caterpillar but engage
in the beauty of a colorful butterfly. Show
your beauty and what you can do.

Quoted By: Doris Freeman (Sister Love)

FEBRUARY 19

John 15:16 "I appointed you to go and
bear fruit. Fruit that will last."

Blessings are hanging like fruit on a tree. Reach high
and grab some. Be thankful. Now make things happen.

Quoted By: Doris Freeman (Sister Love)

FEBRUARY 20

John 11:25 "Jesus said to her, I am the resurrection and the life. The one who believes in me will live even though they die."

However, you live your life, is how you will be remembered in the afterlife.

Quoted By: Doris Freeman (Sister Love)

FEBRUARY 21

Psalm 100:5 "For the Lord is good. His unfailing love continues forever, and his faithfulness continues to each generation."

There is no greater expression of love and generosity than the one that continues for generation after generation and through eternity.

Quoted By: Doris Freeman (Sister Love)

FEBRUARY 22

Isaiah 43:2 "When you go through deep waters, I will be with you. When you go through rivers of difficulty, you will not drown."

Just because the water gets deep, it does not mean you are going to drown. God is holding you hand the entire time.

Quoted By: Doris Freeman (Sister Love)

FEBRUARY 23

Psalm 138:3 "When we get overwhelmed and start feeling down, God will hear our prayers and give us strength. How nice it is to have that strength to lean on during hard times."

Life is like a roller coaster. It takes you on dips and turns and around and around, yet it brings you down to safety for you to keep moving.

Quoted By: Doris Freeman (Sister Love)

FEBRUARY 24

Psalms 46:1 "God is our refugee and strength,
a very present help in trouble."

No matter what you are going through in
life, never give up. Keep pushing, better
days and bigger blessings are coming.

Quoted By: Doris Freeman (Sister Love)

FEBRUARY 25

Proverbs 16:28 "A dishonest man spreads strife, and a whisperer separates close friends"

Stay clear of our enemies. Stay close to your friends. Make a bond that will never end.

Quoted By: Doris Freeman (Sister Love)

FEBRUARY 26

Ecclesiastes 4:10 "If either of them falls down, one will help the other up. But pity anyone who falls and has no one to help them up."

A true friend will not leave you in the time of storms. They stay and ride the waves with you.

Quoted By: Doris Freeman (Sister Love)

FEBRUARY 27

Jeremiah 20:11 "I will put an everlasting reproach on you and an everlasting humiliation which will not be forgotten."

When blessings come, do not forget who got you there. (GOD)

Quoted By: Doris Freeman (Sister Love)

FEBRUARY 28

Proverbs 14:30 "A heart at peace gives life
to the body, but envy rots the bones."

Be happy and thankful with what you have, not what
you see someone else has. Jealousy is not a good spirit.

Quoted By: Doris Freeman (Sister Love)

FEBRUARY 29

Colossians 3:14 "And over all these virtues put on love, which binds them all together in perfect unity."

Today is a new day. Let us exhale all the evil, hatred, and prejudices. Inhale hope, love, and togetherness. One nation, under God, and justice for all. Take the leap of faith.

Quoted By: Doris Freeman (Sister Love)

MARCH 1

Proverbs 21:5 "The thoughts of the diligent
tend only to plenteousness; but of every
one that is hasty only to want."

Be diligent in thoughts for reaching your goal
You may be the first to claim your role
Haste without thoroughness may lead to stagnation
Steadfast persistence reaps a triumphant sensation

Contributed by: Debra Domino

MARCH 2

Timothy 2:15 "Study to shew thyself approved unto God, a workman that needeth not to be ashamed, rightly dividing the word of truth."

Study and read books to grow and find clarity
Knowledge and wisdom mend the disparity
Understanding and application be thyself approved
Empowered by the works and worth of your groove

Contributed by: Debra Domino

MARCH 3

Hebrews 4:12 "For the word of God is alive and active. Sharper than any double-edged sword, it penetrates even to dividing soul and spirit, joints and marrow; it judges the thoughts and attitudes of the heart."

Words are powerful and can cut like a knife
Penetrating and causing conflict and strife
Thoughts before speaking can rescind the attack
Attitudes of the heart control what you attract

Contributed by: Debra Domino

MARCH 4

Titus 3:14 "Our people must learn to devote themselves to doing what is good, in order to provide for urgent needs and not live unproductive lives."

Doing something worthy is very productive

Serving the most urgent needs is constructive

Devotion to what is critical and necessary provides

Goodwill and support that help many lives

Contributed by: Debra Domino

Colossians 3:2 "Set your minds on things
above, not on earthly things."

Focus on the thoughts of your own affection
Deep inside is the compass for your direction
Building the frame of your mindset
Can be the key to a necessary reset

Contributed by: Debra Domino

Corinthians 12:14-20 "¹⁴Even so the body is not made up of one part but of many. ¹⁵Now if the foot should say, Because I am not a hand, I do not belong to the body," it would not for that reason stop being part of the body. ¹⁶And if the ear should say, "Because I am not an eye, I do not belong to the body," it would not for that reason stop being part of the body. ¹⁷If the whole body were an eye, where would the sense of hearing be? If the whole body were an ear, where would the sense of smell be? ¹⁸But in fact God has placed the parts in the body, every one of them, just as he wanted them to be. ¹⁹If they were all one part, where would the body be? ²⁰As it is, there are many parts, but one body."

Co-existence with broad-mindedness
let the story be told

The many parts work together to
make the sum of the whole

Every branch is needed for good reasons of plenty

For it all comes together as one body to serve many

Contributed by: Debra Domino

MARCH 7

Samuel 22:7 "In my distress I called upon the Lord,
Yes, I cried to my God; And from His temple He heard
my voice, and my cry for help came into His ears.

Humbly raise your voice in need to be heard
A sincere prayer is the greatest spoken word
Crying out in the time of need and distress
May the ears of help answer as you confess

Contributed by: Debra Domino

MARCH 8

Psalm 139:14 "I praise you because I am
fearfully and wonderfully made; your works
are wonderful, I know that full well."

International women's day is one of honor
A time to accelerate the exceptional works of wonder
The miracles wonderfully made well to celebrate
The achievements of empowerment
to forever commemorate

Contributed by: Debra Domino

MARCH 9

Romans 15:1-2 "We who are strong ought to bear with the failings of the weak and not to please ourselves. [2]Each of us should please our neighbors for their good, to build them up."

Strength building is a team effort of
support and understanding
Being considerate with patience
without being demanding
Those who are strong lend hands to help the weak
The effort is to lift up others and not for fame to seek

Contributed by: Debra Domino

MARCH 10

Exodus 9:16 "But I have raised you up, Or
"have spared you" for this very purpose, that I
might show you my power and that my name
might be proclaimed in all the earth."

The discovery of who you are and your purpose to give
Is the reason for the miracle of life granted to live
To be born and anointed with the power to proclaim
The authority and the glory to call out his name

Contributed by: Debra Domino

Joshua 1:9 "Have I not commanded you? Be strong and courageous. Do not be afraid; do not be discouraged, for the LORD your God will be with you wherever you go."

Lean into your fears to find the courage to stand
It is within your power to listen to the command
Do not be discouraged and always know
That God will be with you wherever you go

Contributed by: Debra Domino

MARCH 12

Isaiah 40:8 "The grass withers and the flowers fall, but the word of our God endures forever."

Though the grass withers and the flowers fall
A new season arrives and trees grow tall
Beautiful flowers blossom and sprouts of grass spread
To acknowledge and reaffirm that the seed is not dead

Contributed by: Debra Domino

MARCH 13

Proverbs 20:15 "There is gold, and a multitude of rubies: but the lips of knowledge are a precious jewel."

The precious jewels sparkle bright each day
Brimming with wisdom and wanting to say
The value stored inside is more valuable than gold
The power of knowledge is the finest gem to hold

Contributed by: Debra Domino

Kings 7:23 "He made the Sea of cast metal,
circular in shape, measuring ten cubits from
rim to rim and five cubits high. It took a line
of thirty cubits to measure around it."

The math of the formula Pi infinitely grows
The value of a pie can be more than anyone knows
Like the sea circling and flowing with large capability
Your own circle of wealth may be an endowed facility

Contributed by: Debra Domino

MARCH 15

Proverbs 28:13 "He who conceals his transgressions will not prosper, but he who confesses and forsakes them will find compassion."

To thine self be true and make it known in confession
Acknowledge and own up to an offensive transgression
Reconciliation and absolution in the quest you may find
Compassion and cleansing with a peaceful state of mind

Contributed by: Debra Domino

MARCH 16

Peter 3:3 "Your beauty should not come from outward adornment, such as elaborate hairstyles and the wearing of gold jewelry or fine clothes.

Inner beauty shines outward like pure gold
A gentle and quiet spirit is magnificent to behold
The unfading beauty stunning and naturally worn
The authentic inner-self is the greatest to adorn

Contributed by: Debra Domino

MARCH 17

James 1:17 "Every good and perfect gift is from above, coming down from the Father of the heavenly lights, who does not change like shifting shadows."

Luck and blessings make a great gift
May this day bring good luck to give you a lift
Every good and perfect gift is from above
To surround you and protect you with God's love

Contributed by: Debra Domino

MARCH 18

Ezekiel 32:7 "When I snuff you out, I will cover the heavens and darken their stars; I will cover the sun with a cloud, and the moon will not give its light."

The alignment of the sun, moon, and earth is ecliptic
Obscuring of light with the allure of darkness is prolific
A short pause with a shadow to reveal a new moon
A new array of sunshine revealing a breakthrough soon

Contributed by: Debra Domino

Romans 2:7 "To those who by persistence
in doing good seek glory, honor and
immortality, he will give eternal life."

Honor those who give promise and
persistence without neglect

Brotherly love is a principle of
devotion that deserves respect

Doing good for others is an admirable ethic of morality

The inherent of the inheritance has a life of immortality

Contributed by: Debra Domino

MARCH 20

Isaiah 12:3 "With joy you will draw
water from the wells of salvation."

Happiness is a resource that can turn a sad to a glad
The well of salvation can bring the joy you never had
Deliverance that the world cannot give or say
Unspeakable joy that cannot be taken away

Contributed by: Debra Domino

MARCH 21

Colossians 3:21 "Fathers, do not embitter your
children, or they will become discouraged."

Parenting is a gift that takes patience to master
Children look up their parents to learn and grow faster
A bitter parent can discourage and suppress
The growth and spirit of a child's progress

Contributed by: Debra Domino

MARCH 22

Hebrews 10:22 "Let us draw near with a true
heart in full assurance of faith, having our
hearts sprinkled from an evil conscience, and
our bodies washed with pure water."

Water is symbolic of purity and vitality
It is essential for life's renewal and fertility
A true faithful heart assures that the water will flow
To wash away all evil and the reflection will show

Contributed by: Debra Domino

MARCH 23

Proverbs 27:19 "As water reflects the face,
so one's life reflects the heart."

The reflection of your life is the heart's revelation
Ups and downs through trials and tribulations
Does the face reflect the passion of your actions?
Let your story be told to your own satisfaction

Contributed by: Debra Domino

MARCH 24

Isaiah 28:16 "So this is what the Sovereign LORD says: "See, I lay a stone in Zion, a tested stone, a precious cornerstone for a sure foundation; the one who relies on it will never be stricken with panic.

The foundation stands firm with a solid cornerstone
Trusting gives confidence that will always be shown
A solid rock tested to guard against panic attacks
A wall built to last that will always have your back

Contributed by: Debra Domino

MARCH 25

Psalm 103:6 "The LORD executes righteousness
and justice for all the oppressed."

May the word of God invoke justice for the oppressed

May the unjust be enriched with spiritual awareness

May the righteousness uphold with
decency and morality

Peace and justice with fairness and nobility

Contributed by: Debra Domino

MARCH 26

Ecclesiastes 9:7 "Go, eat your food with gladness,
and drink your wine with a joyful heart, for
God has already approved what you do."

Today is one to enjoy food to nourish your health
A joyful and merry heart also promotes wealth
Give yourself approval to be happy with pleasure
Savor and cherish the moment to treasure

Contributed by: Debra Domino

MARCH 27

Isaiah 64:8 "But now, O LORD, thou art our
father; we are the clay, and thou our potter;
and we all are the work of thy hand."

Today is one to inspire with artistic creations
The works of thy hand and mind make formations
To inspire imagination and inventive abstracts
To design masterpieces that fascinate and attract

Contributed by: Debra Domino

MARCH 28

Song of Solomon 2:12-13 "Flowers appear on the earth; the season of singing has come, the cooing of doves is heard in our land. [13]The fig tree forms its early fruit; the blossoming vines spread their fragrance. Arise, come, my darling; my beautiful one, come with me."

Spring's fragrant blossoms add beauty to the season
Earth's gifts of life give promise and the reason
To arise and sing like birds with hope and glee
Enjoy the early fruit hanging from the tree

Contributed by: Debra Domino

MARCH 29

Daniel 8:27 "Daniel, was worn out. I lay
exhausted for several days. Then I got up and
went about the king's business. I was appalled
by the vision; it was beyond understanding."

Make business plans with dedication and accountability
Visualize with strategies to move forward responsibly
Exhaustion may come but faith makes possibilities
The progress achieved can make visions realities

Contributed by: Debra Domino

MARCH 30

Luke 5:31 "Jesus answered them, "It is not the healthy who need a doctor, but the sick."

Pray and send positive thoughts to the sick in need
Physical and mental wellness help the soul to feed
Nourishment for health and wellness indeed
Bless the hands of the doctors to care and take heed

Contributed by: Debra Domino

MARCH 31

Corinthians 3:6-9 "planted the seed, Apollos watered it, but God has been making it grow. [7]So neither the one who plants nor the one who waters is anything, but only God, who makes things grow. [8]The one who plants and the one who waters have one purpose, and they will each be rewarded according to their own labor. [9]For we are co-workers in God's service; you are God's field, God's building."

Planting and watering are labors
with purpose and rapport

The agriculture promotes the
production for needed support

Co-workers in service demonstrate
the works of life's best

The reward for the labor is growth,
prosperity, and success

Contributed by: Debra Domino

APRIL 1

**Welcome to the midpoint of
the first half of the year!**

Psalm 101:7 "No one who practices deceit
shall dwell in my house; no one who utters
lies shall continue before my eyes."

April 1ˢᵗ is a day of jokes and hoaxes usually
carried out with fun and humorous intent. May
this day be filled with laughs and innocent
fun and not with malicious deceit.

Contributed by: Debra Domino

Matthew 7:12 "So in everything do to others what you would have them do to you, for this sums up the Law and the Prophets."

They fooled you once, fooled you twice
You fool them and they say you're not nice
Lessons learned if friend or foe
The truth revealed can be a big blow

Contributed By: Debra Domino

Psalm 119:105 "Your word is a lamp
unto my feet, a light on my path."

Walk proudly in the light of your own pace
It is you who decides the speed of your race
Remember it is not just about the swift
But the lasting endurance that powers the lift

Contributed by: Debra Domino

APRIL 4

John 3:8 "The wind blows wherever it pleases.
You hear its sound, but you cannot tell where
it comes from or where it is going. So it is
with everyone born of the Spirit."

The rustle of the leaves as the wind makes its flurry

Blowing, whistling, and moving in a hurry

Feeling the breeze and hearing the sound

An invisible companion is all around

Contributed by: Debra Domino

APRIL 5

Proverbs 21:21 "He who pursues righteousness
and loyalty Finds life, righteousness
and honor. God is loyal to us."

The loyalty of a good friend is like gold
A diamond to treasure that never grows old
Finding and keeping the honor earned
Is a lifestyle of giving loyalty in return

Contributed by: Debra Domino

APRIL 6

Psalms 5:11 "But let all who take refuge in
you be glad; let them ever sing for joy. Spread
your protection over them, that those who
love your name may rejoice in you."

Another day of beauty to feel good and be glad
To sing a song of joy that uplifts the sad
Giving thanks for the goodwill and protection
Rejoice in the moment of love and perfection

Contributed by: Debra Domino

APRIL 7

Proverbs 16:24 "Pleasant words are as a honeycomb, sweet to the soul, and health to the bones."

Healing begins with speaking words that are kind
The effects of compassion can be soothing to the mind
Feeling the sweet thoughts like communion to the soul
The ambiance for humanity to have and to hold

Contributed by: Debra Domino

APRIL 8

Thessalonians 5:18 "When we find ourselves
overwhelmed with burdens and worried about
tomorrow, we can praise God for who he is and
his promise to never leave us or forsake us."

Even when times seem tough
Whatever you have is just enough
Embrace what you have with love and share
Enjoy life and show how much you care

Contributed by: Debra Domino

APRIL 9

Psalm: 17:7 Show me the wonders of your great love, you who save by your right hand those who take refuge in you from their foes. Shew thy marvelous loving kindness, O thou that savest by thy right hand them which put their trust in thee from those that rise up against them.

Obstacles come and make the mind ponder
Next steps unseen left to wonder
Right by your side works the right hand
It becomes clear what's the next stand

Contributed by: Debra Domino

APRIL 10

John 4:20 – If a man says, I love God, and
hateth his brother, he is a liar: for he that loveth
not his brother whom he hath seen, how can
he love God whom he hath not seen?

Brothers and Sisters from the same or another Mother
The love inspired is like none other
Born to support through the seen and unseen
Love, Mercy, and Dominion give the shoulders to lean

Contributed by: Debra Domino

APRIL 11

James 3:17 "But the wisdom from above is first pure, then peaceable, gentle, open to reason, full of mercy and good fruits, impartial and sincere."

Savor in the moment of fresh fruit of season
Sincere and peaceful thoughts are open to reason
Let the labor of your intentions plant the seed
Goodness, Grace, and Mercy give the call to heed

Contributed by: Debra Domino

APRIL 12

Proverbs 15:13 "A heart full of joy and goodness
makes a cheerful face, But when a heart is
full of sadness the spirit is crushed."

Nurture your thoughts to sooth and calm
Mental practice can be a healing balm
A positive mindset frames the perfect place
To align each heartbeat with a cheerful face

Contributed by: Debra Domino

APRIL 13

Ephesians 2:7 "In order that in the coming ages he
might show the incomparable riches of his grace,
expressed in his kindness to us in Christ Jesus."

Simple acts of expression can mean so much
A smile, a hug, a gesture with a kind touch
Benevolent acts are riches to express and show
The love of God's grace for all to know

Contributed by: Debra Domino

APRIL 14

Isaiah 58:11 "The LORD will guide you always; he will satisfy your needs in a sun-scorched land and will strengthen your frame. You will be like a well-watered garden, like a spring whose waters never fail."

Days of suffering may seem like a drought
Just in time the spring upwells a spout
Streaming and sprinkling quenching the thirst
Like an emergency responder showing up first

Contributed by: Debra Domino

APRIL 15

Peter 5:9 "Whom resist steadfast in the faith, knowing that the same afflictions are accomplished in your brethren that are in the world."

Stand firm in your belief and remain steadfast
Persistent determination gives the will to outlast
The afflictions of hardships stirring and brewing
Brethren united in faith moving and shewing

Contributed by: Debra Domino

APRIL 16

Romans 12:2 "And be not conformed to this world: but be ye transformed by the renewing of your mind, that ye may prove what [is] that good, and acceptable, and perfect, will of God."

Battles of the world are always occurring
Your mind is the fortress for preparing and conferring
Daily affirmations of what's good and acceptable
Provide renewal and strength to supply your receptacle

Contributed by: Debra Domino

APRIL 17

Psalm 72:6 "May he be like rain falling on a mown field, like showers watering the earth."

Showers may rain down covering the lawn
Glistening like dew amidst the sparkle of dawn
Droplets of water cleansing the earth
Restoring and healing for a new birth

Contributed by: Debra Domino

APRIL 18

Song of Solomon 2:3 "Like an apple tree
among the trees of the forest is my beloved
among the young men. I delight to sit in his
shade, and his fruit is sweet to my taste."

Trees of the forest produce fruit of plenty
The roots of good stock to birth and grow many
Golden and delicious to taste and to pleasure
The sweetness of life's journey to live and to treasure

Contributed by: Debra Domino

APRIL 19

Luke 6:21 "Blessed are you who hunger now,
for you will be satisfied. Blessed are you
who weep now, for you will laugh."

Hunger and thirst are not only about food
Craving of any desire can affect your mood
Emotions may arouse and cause you to weep
The satisfaction of laughter is the antidote to keep

Contributed by: Debra Domino

APRIL 20

Proverbs 17:22 "A cheerful heart is good medicine,
but a crushed spirit dries up the bones."

Many remedies are taken to give the day a jumpstart
The best medicine for feeling good is a cheerful heart
A crushed spirit can damage the body and the mind
An attitude of faith and love is the best medicine to find

Contributed by: Debra Domino

APRIL 21

Proverbs 16:3 "Commit your works to the
Lord And your plans will be established."

Order your thoughts with an open mind free of muddle
Organize your work station and clear off all clutter
Commit yourself to efforts that support your resolve
Stay grounded in your beliefs and your plans will evolve

Contributed by: Debra Domino

APRIL 22

Psalm 96: 11-12 "Let the heavens rejoice, let the earth be glad; let the sea resound, and all that is in it. [12]Let the fields be jubilant, and everything in them; let all the trees of the forest sing for joy."

Rejoice be glad and revel with mirth
Today is one to celebrate this great Earth
May the environment breathe clean air that's pure
Let Mother Earth resound and deliver the cure

Contributed by: Debra Domino

Isaiah 1:17 "Learn to do right; seek justice. Defend the oppressed. Take up the cause of the fatherless; plead the case of the widow. Learn to do right; seek justice."

Trouble on the journey can make life distressed

Learn to seek justice to defend the oppressed

Truthfulness and fairness stand for righteousness

Your heart will guide you to do what's best

Contributed by: Debra Domino

APRIL 24

Matthew 23:25-28 "Woe to you, scribes and Pharisees, hypocrites! For you clean the outside of the cup and of the dish, but inside they are full of robbery and self-indulgence. You blind Pharisee, first clean the inside of the cup and of the dish, so that the outside of it may become clean also."

Contriteness from the inside can show on the outside
What's written over your face is hard to hide
Self-cleansing begins from inside to the surface
Eradicating is a massive task to efface

Contributed by: Debra Domino

APRIL 25

Psalm 139:13-16 "[13]For you created my inmost being; you knit me together in my mother's womb. [14]I praise you because I am fearfully and wonderfully made; your works are wonderful, I know that full well. [15]My frame was not hidden from you when I was made in the secret place, when I was woven together in the depths of the earth. [16]Your eyes saw my unformed body; all the days ordained for me were written in your book before one of them came to be."

Today is one to think about the many unique designs
From the earth to the womb woven and intertwined
The making of all the works formed and framed
Ordained and marvelous before being named

Contributed by: Debra Domino

APRIL 26

Proverbs 12:10 "Whoever is righteous has regard for the life of his beast, but the mercy of the wicked is cruel."

Both human and animal life deserve kindness
Evil acts of wickedness are mean and merciless
Cruelty shows vicious and malicious neglect
The righteous show regard for benevolent respect

Contributed by: Debra Domino

APRIL 27

Matthew 13:1-5 "That same day Jesus went out of the house and sat by the lake. ²Such large crowds gathered around him that he got into a boat and sat in it, while all the people stood on the shore. ³Then he told them many things in parables, saying: "A farmer went out to sow his seed. ⁴As he was scattering the seed, some fell along the path, and the birds came and ate it up. ⁵Some fell on rocky places, where it did not have much soil. It sprang up quickly, because the soil was shallow.

Parables roll out each day that teach and guide
Giving meaning to life's experiences for you to abide
Each new day is a chapter in life's great book
Write your story today and brand your unique hook

Contributed by: Debra Domino

APRIL 28

Corinthians 16:13-14 "Be on your guard;
stand firm in the faith; be courageous; be
strong. [14]Do everything in love."

There comes a time when you have to stand to attention
Be the guard of the destiny that holds your intention
Standing firm in faith gives the strength to be brave
The power of love brings the necessary save

Contributed by: Debra Domino

Psalm 149:3-4 "Let them praise his name with dancing and make music to him with timbrel and harp. [4]For the LORD takes delight in his people; he crowns the humble with victory."

Each new experience can be like a partner in a dance
The melody of the music prepares
you to take your stance
The rhythm, the movement, the attitude to claim
The humble victory and praise symbolic of his name

Contributed by: Debra Domino

Genesis 9:11-16 "I establish my covenant with you: Never again will all life be destroyed by the waters of a flood; never again will there be a flood to destroy the earth." [12]And God said, "This is the sign of the covenant I am making between me and you and every living creature with you, a covenant for all generations to come: [13]I have set my rainbow in the clouds, and it will be the sign of the covenant between me and the earth. [14]Whenever I bring clouds over the earth and the rainbow appears in the clouds, [15]I will remember my covenant between me and you and all living creatures of every kind. Never again will the waters become a flood to destroy all life. [16]Whenever the rainbow appears in the clouds, I will see it and remember the everlasting covenant between God and all living creatures of every kind on the earth."

Storms may come with the appearance of a dark cloud

There is a promise to cover with a protective shroud

The covenant is made for all the world to know

The sign is the colorful arc of the rainbow

Contributed by: Debra Domino

MAY 1

Psalms 133:1-3 "How good and pleasant it is when God's people live together in unity! [2]It is like precious oil poured on the head, running down on the beard, running down on Aaron's beard, down on the collar of his robe. [3]It is as if the dew of Hermon were falling on Mount Zion."

May 1 is a day to join together in the spirit of unity
Living together peacefully in the community
Soothing like precious oil and the sound of a symphony
It is good when God's people live together in harmony

Contributed by: Debra Domino

1 John 4:20-21 "If someone claims, "I love God," but hates his brother or sister, then he is a liar. Anyone who does not love a brother or sister, whom he has seen, cannot possibly love God, whom he has never seen. [21]He gave us a clear command, that all who love God must also love their brothers and sisters."

Siblings are the deepest expression
that connect family love

Like the pure essence of conflict and
reconcile symbolic of the dove

Siblings can grow and work together
like links in a stable chain

The bonds shared for a lifetime when
broken are never the same

Contributed by: Debra Domino

MAY 3

Isaiah 26:3 "You will keep in perfect peace those whose minds are steadfast, because they trust in you."

Meditate upon calmness with relaxation and peace
Focus on the perfect mental space to make anxiety cease
Mental stimulation helps balance the body's interactions
Trusting the impulse to let go of distractions

Contributed by: Debra Domino

MAY 4

Timothy 1:6 For this reason I remind you to kindle afresh the gift of God which is in you through the laying on of my hands."

"May the Fourth Be With You"

Today is one to refresh the reason for your spark
Light it up removing any feelings that are dark
The kindle is your gift for whatever you want to do
Through you and in you, may the fourth be with you

Contributed by: Debra Domino

MAY 5

Timothy 4:16 "Take heed unto thyself, and unto the doctrine; continue in them: for in doing this thou shalt both save thyself, and them that hear thee."

Mindfulness is the consciousness of being aware
Take heed in attending to your own self-care
In doing so shall save thyself and the hearer
Hearing what's emerging makes seeing it clearer

Contributed by: Debra Domino

MAY 6

Job 22:27 "You will pray to him, and he will hear you, and you will fulfill your vows."

Today is a good day to communicate
a sincere prayer request
It is the plea for grace and mercy and for the bequest
The honest asking from the heart
brings comfort and rapport
That the portal is always open to render support

Contributed by: Debra Domino

MAY 7

Proverbs 31:25-27" King James Version (KJV)
25Strength and honour are her clothing; and she
shall rejoice in time to come. 26She openeth her
mouth with wisdom; and in her tongue is the law
of kindness. 27She looketh well to the ways of her
household, and eateth not the bread of idleness."

The many cloths a Mother wears are heroic and fearless

Valor, strength, boldness, unselfishness,
kind, and dearest

Mothers speak triumph through victory and pain

The honor of a Mother is the greatest honor to obtain

Contributed by: Debra Domino

MAY 8

Luke 11:41 "But now as for what is
inside you-be generous to the poor, and
everything will be clean for you."

Giving is the gift of charity of what is inside
Your generous offering is like a flow of the tide
The wave of blessings starts a surge of support
The benefit flows back for consent and rapport

Contributed by: Debra Domino

MAY 9

Ephesians 6:15 "And with your feet fitted with the readiness that comes from the gospel of peace."

Preparedness comes with being
attentive and getting ready

The fitting of the right shoes for
moving and staying steady

To spread the good news about the gospel of peace

The announcement about armistice
and the conflict will cease

Contributed by: Debra Domino

MAY 10

Psalm 51:10 "Create in me a clean heart, O God, and renew a right spirit within me."

Housekeeping and daily maintenance
require ongoing cleanings

The upkeep relating to cleaning has
many different meanings

The first place to begin is created within the heart

Renewal of the right spirit is how the clean-up starts

Contributed by: Debra Domino

MAY 11

Luke 11:52 "'Woe unto you lawyers! for
ye have taken away the key of knowledge:
ye entered not in yourselves, and them
that were entering in ye hindered."

One side another side, but the truth lies in the middle
A battle of choosing which side clouds the riddle
The key of knowledge is in the center of the facts
Integrity and honesty are needed
for the verdict to be exact

Contributed by: Debra Domino

MAY 12

Timothy 5:8 "But if any provide not for his own, and especially for those of his own house, he hath denied the faith, and is worse than an infidel."

Set your own standards for yourself
and your family's care

Attentiveness to the primary and
crucial needs is being aware

Adhere to your own faith and may your home be secure

Providing for your own is the
foundation to build and procure

Contributed by: Debra Domino

MAY 13

Luke 11:21-22 "When a strong man, fully armed, guards his own house, his possessions are safe. [22]But when someone stronger attacks and overpowers him, he takes away the armor in which the man trusted and divides up his plunder."

Weapons of destruction attract bigger
weapons to cause harm

A force meant to protect can be
overpowered and disarmed

Open carrying to fire has no rules and no cease

Ongoing and instamatic is an injustice of the peace

Contributed by: Debra Domino

MAY 14

Romans 13:13 "Let us walk with decency,
as in the daylight: not in carousing and
drunkenness; not in sexual impurity and
promiscuity; not in quarreling and jealousy."

A day of decency is a dedication to dignity
A simple act of morality that shows sensibility
Standards and ethics are virtues to demonstrate
For the righteous to show and for others to replicate

Contributed by: Debra Domino

MAY 15

Matthew 5:9 "Blessed are the peacemakers,
for they will be called children of God."

The spreading of good will to bring harmony is chivalry

Peaceful acts and actions from leaders show bravery

Progress during peacetime bring
resolution and reconciliation

All can come together for God's work and emancipation

Contributed by: Debra Domino

MAY 16

Jeremiah 17:8 "They will be like a tree planted by the water that sends out its roots by the stream. It does not fear when heat comes; its leaves are always green. It has no worries in a year of drought and never fails to bear fruit."

Standing firm by the water planting
roots into the stream
Heat can come but leaves will always be green
No fear or worry that branches will wither or lean
A year of drought brings no lack of fruit to be seen

Contributed by: Debra Domino

MAY 17

Psalm 91:11 "The LORD shall preserve
thy going out and thy coming in from this
time forth, and even for evermore."

Traveling near or far deserves grace with preservation

May the Lord guide and guard to each destination

Going out and coming in from
this time forth and ahead

The command to protect from
harm, the order to be lead

Contributed by: Debra Domino

MAY 18

Matthew 25:40 "Truly I tell you, whatever
you did for one of the least of these brothers
and sisters of mine, you did for me."

Hospitality is a cordial way to visit, welcome, and meet
Extending care and support is a loving way to greet
Visits with family and friends can inform and enlighten
A day of communion and fellowship
can uplift and brighten

Contributed by: Debra Domino

MAY 19

Ecclesiastes 11:6 "Sow your seed in the morning and do not be idle in the evening, for you do not know whether morning or evening sowing will succeed, or whether both of them alike will be good."

A day of planting something into fertile ground
Sow your seeds as you make your morning round
Let your heart and impulse guide where to take root
Morning or evening will succeed in the yielding of fruit

Contributed by: Debra Domino

MAY 20

Matthew 6:28 "And why do you worry
about clothes? See how the flowers of the
field grow. They do not labor or spin."

Feel like a millionaire, let your inner glow flow
Like the flowers of the field ready to grow and show
Don't worry about designer clothes just feel the success
Relax, feel the energy, and let your
natural essence progress

Contributed by: Debra Domino

MAY 21

Proverbs 17:27 "A man of knowledge
restrains his words, and a man of
understanding maintains a calm spirit."

Knowledge carries much power yet
it comes with constraint

Knowing how and when to deliver
certain words come with restraint

The intelligence of understanding
and mastering comprehension

The realization that a calm spirit sets the right intention

Contributed by: Debra Domino

MAY 22

Psalm 107:23 "Some went down to the sea in ships, doing business on the great waters"

The daily works from the land to the sea
Filled with the wonders of the water and its mystery
The vast and deep pockets of the ocean's floor
The maritime of life's expeditions and discoveries galore

Contributed by: Debra Domino

MAY 23

Ephesians 1:11 "In him we have obtained an inheritance, having been predestined according to the purpose of him who works all things according to the counsel of his will."

Let your purpose guide you to reveal a great gift
Just in time to give you a very necessary lift
All things work together according to the will
Delivered right on time signed and sealed

Contributed by: Debra Domino

MAY 24

Hebrews 13:1 "Keep on loving one
another as brothers and sisters."

Hope comes with the relationship of brotherhood
The association of Brothers and Sisters
work for the greater good
A stranger in the mist could be an angel in disguise
Loving one another is benevolent and wise

Contributed by: Debra Domino

MAY 25

Romans 12:4 "For just as each of us has one
body with many members, and these members
do not all have the same function."

The body was built with many cells working in action
Serving and working together and gaining traction
To keep the body healthy and ready for fitness
Physical and mental wellness, what
a great state to witness!

Contributed by: Debra Domino

MAY 26

Proverbs 12:25 "Anxiety weighs down the
heart, but a kind word cheers it up."

Be a good cheerleader for your own appease

Anxiety dampens the spirit and causes unease

Kind words for yourself and others can bring cheer

It is soothing for the heart and for your ears to hear

Contributed by: Debra Domino

MAY 27

Psalm 27:3 "Though an army besiege me, my heart
will not fear; though war break out against me,
even then I will be confident. Though a mighty
army surrounds me, my heart will not be afraid."

A great legacy follows the footsteps of bravery
The nobility, courage, and grand acts of chivalry
Thank you for your service to life and mankind
The memory of your contributions will forever shine

Contributed by: Debra Domino

Romans 13:4 "For the one in authority is God's servant for your good. But if you do wrong, be afraid, for rulers do not bear the sword for no reason. They are God's servants, agents of wrath to bring punishment on the wrongdoer."

Human rights are a protection that's also a birthright

Dignity, Respect, Equality, and
Fairness are worth the fight

Amnesty is about helping the
downtrodden and oppressed

The imperative effort necessary for humanity's progress

Contributed by: Debra Domino

MAY 29

Luke 16:10 "Whoever can be trusted with very little can also be trusted with much, and whoever is dishonest with very little will also be dishonest with much."

A small gesture may be the glue that
holds something together

Any act of kindness can be the piece
that strengthens the tether

Like a paper clip that holds the papers in tack

Small but useful to keep things on track

Contributed by: Debra Domino

MAY 30

Isaiah 67:17 "Create in me a pure heart, O God,
and renew a steadfast spirit within me."

A great day to create or do something
pure from the heart
It could be a plan of action to get a fresh start
It could be a new idea conceived in the mind
It could be a new construct of a beautiful design

Contributed by: Debra Domino

MAY 31

Job 9:27 "If I say, 'I will forget my complaint,
I will change my expression, and smile."

Today is one to change the face of
complaint with a smile

A journey begins with one step, and
the smile can radiate for miles

It is because the gesture puts you in
a favorable state of mind

It can change the outlook and leave the negative behind

Contributed by: Debra Domino

JUNE 1

Ephesians 4:29 "Do not let any unwholesome talk come out of your mouths, but only what is helpful for building others up according to their needs, that it may benefit those who listen."

Like the symbolism of the pearl and its purity

Wholesome talk has decency and maturity

Helpful conversation is great communication

Hurtful and harmful attacks are
not good for articulation

Contributed by: Debra Domino

JUNE 2

Proverbs 12: 23-24 "All hard work brings a profit, but mere talk leads only to poverty. [24]The wealth of the wise is their crown, but the folly of fools yields folly."

Hard work is needed to grow and support life
Yet living to only work can add stress and strife
Find the best balance of pleasure and work to abound
Not about mere talk but using the wealth of your crown

Contributed by: Debra Domino

JUNE 3

Hebrews 12:1 "Therefore, since we are surrounded
by such a huge crowd of witnesses to the life of faith,
let us strip off every weight that slows us down,
especially the sin that so easily trips us up. And let us
run with endurance the race God has set before us."

Running for fitness builds up endurance
The staying power is like faith for daily reassurance
Surrounded by crowds and stumbling blocks to trip
God's race is set with fortitude and the promise to equip

Contributed by: Debra Domino

JUNE 4

Samuel 17:18 "And carry these ten cheeses unto
the captain of their thousand, and look how
thy brethren fare, and take their pledge."

A day to celebrate the product named cheese
Coagulated from milk with tastes to please
Metaphoric for making money and also feeding
Supplying thousands of people hungry and needing

Contributed by: Debra Domino

JUNE 5

Genesis 1:26 "Then God said, "Let us make mankind in our image, in our likeness, so that they may rule over the fish in the sea and the birds in the sky, over the livestock and all the wild animals, and over all the creatures that move along the ground."

The beauty of the environment is a
system of energy that flows

The community of living organisms
makes an ecosystem that grows

Mankind created in God's image
and likeness to conserve

The ecology of life's systems and humanity to preserve

Contributed by: Debra Domino

Proverbs 4:13 "Take fast hold of instruction;
let her not go: keep her; for she is thy life."

Instruction and studying are keys to take hold

Education helps with resolutions when life's snags unfold

Being open to continuing learning
things that are new and fast

Becomes a life-long process of
gaining wisdom that will last

Contributed by: Debra Domino

JUNE 7

Isaiah 54:17 "No weapon forged against
you will prevail, and you will refute every
tongue that accuses you. This is the heritage
of the servants of the LORD, and this is their
vindication from me, declares the LORD."

Patience and perseverance are
survival skills for prevailing
Refuting every accuser with vindication entailing
No weapons will prosper is the resounding declaration
It's the heritage for faithful servants and life's affirmation

Contributed by: Debra Domino

JUNE 8

Proverbs 18:24 "One who has unreliable
friends soon comes to ruin, but there is a
friend who sticks closer than a brother."

Being a friend means giving and supporting one another
It doesn't matter if you are a brother
from another mother
The order of friendship is to stick closely together
A comrade, a champion, a collaborator, forever

Contributed by: Debra Domino

JUNE 9

Corinthians 8:14 "At this present time your
abundance being a supply for their need, so
that their abundance also may become a supply
for your need, that there may be equality"

Reciprocity is a mutual interchange of supply
Returning a favor makes the trade multiply
The exchange of resources may increase the quantity
Of abundance for all with fairness and equality

Contributed by: Debra Domino

JUNE 10

Ephesians 5:18 "Do not get drunk on wine, which leads to debauchery. Instead, be filled with the Spirit."

Eating and drinking of spirits can be merry and joyous

The act of over consumption can be tumultuous

Debauchery and drunkenness the overuse can cause

The essence that fills the spirit can stimulate and rouse

Contributed by: Debra Domino

JUNE 11

Genesis 41:5-7 "He fell asleep again and had a second dream: Seven heads of grain, healthy and good, were growing on a single stalk. ⁶After them, seven other heads of grain sprouted-thin and scorched by the east wind. ⁷The thin heads of grain swallowed up the seven healthy, full heads. Then Pharaoh woke up; it had been a dream."

Dreams are visions whether awake or in a sleep state
The revelation of something purposeful
to come can emanate
The dream of being something good and great
What's seen and believed could sprout up and replicate

Contributed by: Debra Domino

JUNE 12

Philippians 1:7 "It is right for me to feel this way
about all of you, since I have you in my heart and,
whether I am in chains or defending and confirming
the gospel, all of you share in God's grace with me."

Acknowledging or celebrating a special day of reflection
Is the greatest expression of appreciation
for another's affection
The feelings are confirmations of the love in your heart
All that has been shared with God's
grace will never part

Contributed by: Debra Domino

JUNE 13

Psalm 127:3 "Children are a heritage from the
LORD, offspring a reward from him."

Children begin the heritage of the new generation
Birth announcements bring joy and celebration
Off springs from God, the legacy continues to grow
Reaping rewards ongoing into the future to sow

Contributed by: Debra Domino

JUNE 14

Psalm 20:5 "May we shout for joy over your salvation, and in the name of our God set up our banners! May the Lord fulfill all your petitions!"

Waving a flag or banner is a special way

To express the significance of
something memorable today

May the banner shout the joy of
what salvation will bring

With the fulfillment of all petitions to let freedom ring

Contributed by: Debra Domino

JUNE 15

Galatians 5:1 "New International Version (NIV) 53 Take possession of the land and settle in it, for I have given you the land to possess. 54 Distribute the land by lot, according to your clans. To a larger group give a larger inheritance, and to a smaller group a smaller one. Whatever falls to them by lot will be theirs."

The grant from God is to distribute the land to live

The larger the group the larger the lot to give

Whatever falls around the lot will be theirs to retain

The inheritance is to build wealth
for the family to sustain

Contributed by: Debra Domino

JUNE 16

Ecclesiastes 11:9 "You who are young, be happy while you are young, and let your heart give you joy in the days of your youth. Follow the ways of your heart and whatever your eyes see, but know that for all these things God will bring you into judgment."

Youthful days are happy and open to educate
Be happy and let the heart shine and radiate
Young with much abundance to give and validate
Strong abilities and ideas to offer and demonstrate

Contributed by: Debra Domino

JUNE 17

Psalm 128:2 "You will eat the fruit of your labor; blessings and prosperity will be yours."

A day to experiment with tasty vegetable dishes
Savoring the fruits of your labor can be delicious
Grilling, salads, stir fry, casseroles, and more
Nutritious recipes can make your prosperity soar

Contributed by: Debra Domino

JUNE 18

Mathew 13:47 "Once again, the kingdom of
heaven is like a net that was let down into
the lake and caught all kinds of fish."

Fishing is an activity of skill and some
make it a sporting match

For recreation or for food it takes
strategy to pull a great catch

Learning the art of fishing like all
quests takes preparation

Connecting and studying patterns
with patient observation

Contributed by: Debra Domino

JUNE 19

Galatians 5:1 "Stand fast therefore in the liberty
wherewith Christ hath made us free, and be not
entangled again with the yoke of bondage."

Stand fast in the liberty of freedom from oppression

Do not be entangled by the yoke of suppression

The burden of slavery is cruel and spiteful domination

Guard your freedom and do not submit to subjugation

Celebrate the Emancipation!

Contributed by: Debra Domino

JUNE 20

2 Corinthians 6:18 "And I will be a father
to you, and you shall be sons and daughters
to me, says the Lord Almighty."

A father is a founder of the family, the patriarch

Partnered with the mother, the co-
founder and matriarch

The Father is meant to influence,
and guide with intellect

Anointed by the almighty to lead and protect

Contributed by: Debra Domino

JUNE 21

Ephesians 5:8 "For you were formerly darkness, but now you are Light in the Lord; walk as children of Light"

The summer solstice is the longest day of light
Walk in the glory of life and behold the sight
Enjoy the beauty of the changing season
Spring into summer with the light of good reason

Contributed by: Debra Domino

JUNE 22

John 8:32 "And you will know the truth,
and the truth will set you free."

The truth of the matter is the reality in plain sight
Sometimes painful or hurtful like a sting or bite
The darkness enlightened to the certainty of fact
The freedom of knowing the truth is a class act

Contributed by: Debra Domino

JUNE 23

Isaiah 1:18 "Come now, and let us reason together,
saith the LORD: though your sins be as scarlet,
they shall be as white as snow; though they be
red like crimson, they shall be as wool."

The expressions of hues give the brilliance of reasons

For decoration and beauty reflected in the seasons

A shade in one degree may change to a different tint

Multiple shades come together to
make a spectacular mint

Contributed by: Debra Domino

JUNE 24

1 Timothy 4:14 "Do not neglect your gift,
which was given you through prophecy when
the body of elders laid their hands on you."

A handshake for a contract or a laying touch
Could be filled with gifts that value much
Do not neglect an insight given by an elder
The prophecy may be worth more than leather

Contributed by: Debra Domino

JUNE 25

Proverbs 13:11 "Dishonest money dwindles away, but whoever gathers money little by little makes it grow."

Industry and economics are like supply and chain
Riskiness and recklessness make for little gain
Methodical planning and analysis encompass
Gradual and steady increases the bold forecast

Contributed by: Debra Domino

JUNE 26

1 Corinthians 6:12 "All things are lawful unto me, but all things are not expedient: all things are lawful for me, but I will not be brought under the power of any."

Respect the law and the duty to do what's necessary
Know that some things may be divergent and contrary
It is left up to your own discern and interpretation
To claim your own power and right of participation

Contributed by: Debra Domino

Psalm 55:22 "Cast your cares on the LORD and he will sustain you; he will never let the righteous be shaken."

Stress can cause pain and emotional trauma
The reason for the episodes can be sparked by drama
The suffering can feel unbearable and unlivable
Cast your burdens to the Lord the savior and deliverer

Contributed by: Debra Domino

JUNE 28

Numbers 4:49 "At the LORD's command
they were numbered through Moses and
each one was assigned his work and burden,
as the LORD had commanded Moses."

Logistics and transportation of
supplies and goods for gains

Carry important responsibilities
for the daily supply chains

The essential services are worth
acknowledgement and celebration

Vital goods and products delivered by
the industry of transportation

Contributed by: Debra Domino

JUNE 29

Genesis 1:26 "Then God said, "Let us make mankind in our image, in our likeness, so that they may rule over the fish in the sea and the birds in the sky, over the livestock and all the wild animals, and over all the creatures that move along the ground."

The Greek meaning of photography
is writing with light

It is a great invention of capturing images in plain sight

The evolution seen from the beginning
of universal creation

To make images of life's likenesses
with a technological innovation

Contributed by: Debra Domino

JUNE 30

Isaiah 35:2 "It shall blossom abundantly
and rejoice with joy and singing."

May the beauty of the June rose kindle joy and patience
The next month of July awaits your mindful presence
For abundant blossoms of growth and insight
Make this next month a great one to highlight

Contributed by: Debra Domino

JULY 1

Ecclesiastes 10:10 "If the axe is dull and the blade unsharpened, more strength must be exerted, but skill produces success. If the ax is dull and its edge unsharpened, more strength is needed, but skill will bring success. Using a dull ax requires great strength, so sharpen the blade. That's the value of wisdom; it helps you succeed."

The day of working is one to applaud
the strength and will
It takes determination to keep
working and building skill
Like a dull blade, skills have to keep being honed
Success is obtained as the wisdom
is sharpened and toned

Contributed by: Debra Domino

JULY 2

Malachi 3:10 "Bring the whole tithe into the storehouse, that there may be food in my house. Test me in this," says the LORD Almighty, "and see if I will not throw open the floodgates of heaven and pour out so much blessing that there will not be room enough to store it."

Contributions of staples build a food bank to store

The tithes and offerings multiply to make much more

The pouring out of donations to help build the reserve

Delivers more blessings to the well deserved

Contributed by: Debra Domino

JULY 3

Ecclesiastes 11:7 "Light is sweet, and it
pleases the eyes to see the sun."

Today may be a bright summer day of the sun
Bathing in its light may seem pleasing and fun
The sweltering heat may require a necessary break
To cool off and regroup for the body's sake

Contributed by: Debra Domino

JULY 4

Psalm 119:45 "I will walk about in freedom,
for I have sought out your precepts."

A day of celebrating the act of owning your own rights

With the freedom to walk and climb to new heights

The precepts are the principles and
commandments to guide the way

For building new foundations and
legacies for independence to stay

Contributed by: Debra Domino

JULY 5

Thessalonians 3:10 "For even when we were
with you, we gave you this rule: "The one who
is unwilling to work shall not eat." (NIV)

Working for causes and for livelihood
are like golden rules
Fruits of labor are like rewards and also tools
Means provide resources producing income for stability
The unwilling defeat the will of their own abilities

Contributed by: Debra Domino

JULY 6

Peter 4:8 "Above all, love each other deeply, because love covers over a multitude of sins."

Today is one to treat yourself to
something of good delight

Give appreciation for everything
around you and in sight

Love covers deeply a multitude of sins

Loving yourself is the opening to
where loving others begins

Contributed by: Debra Domino

Colossians 3:13 "Bear with each other and forgive
one another if any of you has a grievance against
someone. Forgive as the LORD forgave you."

Forgiveness is a voluntary process
given to let go and heal

It may seem weak but it gives
strength to your own appeal

To absolve all grudges and vengeance releases a big gain

Giving cleansing and redemption
while liberating the pain

Contributed by: Debra Domino

JULY 8

Isaiah 17:6 "Yet gleaning grapes shall be left in
it, as the shaking of an olive tree, two or three
berries in the top of the uppermost bough,
four or five in the outmost fruitful branches
thereof, saith the LORD God of Israel."

A summer day to enjoy the fresh fruit of the season

Like the blueberry full of fiber for strength and reason

Gentleness and self-control let the antioxidants roll

Purifying the body and spirit and letting wellness unfold

Contributed by: Debra Domino

JULY 9

Galatians 5:13 – "For, brethren, ye have been called unto liberty; only [use] not liberty for an occasion to the flesh, but by love serve one another."

The call to live is the call to freedom and autonomy
For serving and building up the nation and economy
Beware of back biting and destroying one another
That will prevent your liberty from growing any further

Contributed by: Debra Domino

JULY 10

Isaiah 40:28 – "Hast thou not known? hast thou not heard, that the everlasting God, the LORD, the Creator of the ends of the earth, fainteth not, neither is weary? there is no searching of his understanding."

Energy is an everlasting process to conserve
The earth is a creator holding never ending reserves
The power is not faintest or weary of demanding
The transfer for performance
quantitates the understanding

Contributed by: Debra Domino

JULY 11

Psalm 139:14 – "I praise You, for I am fearfully
and wonderfully made. Marvelous are Your
works, and I know this very well."

Seeing the abilities of all the
attributes of God's creations

Gives the power for each person to
be their own unique sensation

Accepting that your makeup has
been done with a master plan

No disabilities but capabilities to
fulfill the works at hand

Contributed by: Debra Domino

JULY 12

Matthew 6:10 – "Your kingdom come, your
will be done, on earth as it is in heaven."

Each new day gives the opportunity reflect and be still
A time to treasure the simple things
and to do God's will
The kingdom is what you have all around you
It is your heaven on earth to live and make do

Contributed by: Debra Domino

JULY 13

Colossians 2:16 "Therefore do not let anyone judge you by what you eat or drink, or with regard to a religious festival, a New Moon celebration or a Sabbath day."

Celebrate and enjoy delicious cuisines
of your choice and taste

Merrily, let yourself be the judge
of the delight and grace

Festivities are meant to be memorable and extraordinary

Anything less should be left in the
shadows of the contrary

Contributed by: Debra Domino

JULY 14

Psalm 34:18 The LORD is close to the brokenhearted
and saves those who are crushed in spirit."

Alone and crushed inside of a spirit that feels broken
A central space that also stores a special token
A memento that holds a safe to unlock
The save to restore that's solid as a rock

Contributed by: Debra Domino

JULY 15

Corinthians 14:40 "But everything should
be done in a fitting and orderly way."

A day to organize and reduce clutter
Big moves are gradual and subtle
Step by step can create gigantic leaps
Fitting and orderly with benefits to reap

Contributed by: Debra Domino

JULY 16

Revelation 22:5 "And there shall be no night there; and they need no candle, neither light of the sun; for the Lord God giveth them light: and they shall reign for ever and ever."

Summer days bright and sunny beaming with light
The arid summer breeze that fills the night
In the dimmest hour of nightfall's darkest pane
No candle or sun yet the light shall reign

Contributed by: Debra Domino

JULY 17

Timothy 6:18 "That they do good, that
they be rich in good works, ready to
distribute, willing to communicate."

Communication comes in many
forms of work and expression

Emoji's are a modern form of language
but not for suppression

They are facial smileys that give emotional impressions

To send messages with pictorial inflections

Contributed by: Debra Domino

JULY 18

Psalm 36:8 "They feast on the abundance
of Your house, and You give them drink
from Your river of delights"

The simmering summer days are moving with haste

Slow it down and enjoy a delight to charm your taste

It could be a delicious snack or a refreshing drink

A simple feast in the moment can
help you relax and think

Contributed by: Debra Domino

JULY 19

John 14:27 "Peace I leave with you; my peace I give
you. I do not give to you as the world gives. Do not
let your hearts be troubled and do not be afraid."

As you go about your way today focus
on what brings you peace

Let that central focal point guide
you to let go and release

Put your burdens and troubles into that space of exhale

Step out with confidence that a blessing will prevail

Contributed by: Debra Domino

JULY 20

Isaiah 30:26 "The moon will shine like the sun, and the sunlight will be seven times brighter, like the light of seven full days, when the LORD binds up the bruises of his people and heals the wounds he inflicted."

The great companion in the sky shining
during sunset and sunrise

The meaning and mystery of the moon
enthuses romance for the skies

The lunar phases changing faces in
orbit and giving a celestial show

With the sun shining daily bestowing
to earth the heavenly glow

Contributed by: Debra Domino

JULY 21

2 Timothy 1:7 "For God hath not given us the spirit of fear; but of power, and of love, and of a sound mind."

Feel the power of your inner spirit inside and find
Not the spirit of fear but that of a sound mind
Love yourself and the worth that you have to give
Respect yourself and others and
declare your power to live

Contributed by: Debra Domino

JULY 22

Psalm 19:7 "The law of the LORD is perfect,
refreshing the soul. The statutes of the LORD
are trustworthy, making wise the simple"

Refreshing is the quench of thirst on a summer day

Perfect is the refreshment of the soul
to shed light on the way

The trust in the decrees to help make
the difficult seem simple

The wisdom in knowing that steps will be nimble

Contributed by: Debra Domino

JULY 23

Psalm 92:14 NIV "They will still bear fruit in
old age, they will stay fresh and green,"

Grandparents are like natural resources of knowledge

Their years of experience make for a degree in college

Wisdom is an expertise that never grows old

Like a monumental reserve stored with gold

Contributed by: Debra Domino

JULY 24

1 John 4:19 "We love because he first loved us."

After birth, the family love is the first love to see
Siblings and Cousins bond like leaves on a tree
A heart-to-heart relationship connects the family line
Could be the tie that binds friendship for a lifetime

Contributed by: Debra Domino

Proverbs 4:25 "Let your eyes look straight
ahead; fix your gaze directly before you."

Let your eyes guide you to focus on your best
Your worth is about your own individual quest
It is not about the right or left but what's in front of you
It is your destined journey prepared for you to do

Contributed by: Debra Domino

JULY 26

1 Timothy 5:8 "Anyone who does not provide for their relatives, and especially for their own household, has denied the faith and is worse than an unbeliever."

Family support has many different roles

Taking care of the immediate
household is the primary goal

Aunts and Uncles may provide backup support

Their love and wit contribute to the rapport

Contributed by: Debra Domino

JULY 27

Psalm 19:14 "Let the words of my mouth, and the meditation of my heart, be acceptable in thy sight, O LORD, my strength, and my redeemer."

Each spoken word gives an opportunity
to speak a blessing

Each positive word is a way of expressing

The voice of love to be referenced and mentioned

Empowered by the inspiration of
the redeemer's intentions

Contributed by: Debra Domino

JULY 28

Revelations 21:4 "And God shall wipe away all tears from their eyes; and there shall be no more death, neither sorrow, nor crying, neither shall there be any more pain: for the former things are passed away."

Awareness is an important factor
in understanding disease

The pain and suffering that may
come and the prayer for ease

The vision or revelation that illnesses will move away

Perfect health to be restored is the request that we pray

Contributed by: Debra Domino

JULY 29

2 Timothy 3:16 "Then the Lord God formed man of dust from the ground, and breathed into his nostrils the breath of life; and man became a living being."

Air conditioning units are blessings for the summer heat
Like the air of breath sending oxygen
from the head to the feet
Living beings and the accessories
that enhance life's existence
Come together to experience the beauty of subsistence

Contributed by: Debra Domino

JULY 30

Luke 6:45 "A good man brings good things out of the good stored up in his heart, and an evil man brings evil things out of the evil stored up in his heart. For the mouth speaks what the heart is full of."

Speak from your heart with good intentions

Like an elevator speech to sell your inventions

If your heart is full just let it flow

The power of the words could help you grow

Contributed by: Debra Domino

JULY 31

Jeremiah 29:11 "For I know the plans I have for you," declares the Lord, "plans to prosper you and not to harm you, plans to give you hope and a future."

The second month of summer is coming to an end

This a great time to do something wonderful before August begins

It could be the preparation and sharing of a nutritious meal

It could be relaxation or strategizing for a new deal

Contributed by: Debra Domino

AUGUST 1

Ecclesiastes 3:12-13 [12]"I know that there is nothing better for people than to be happy and to do good while they live. [13]That each of them may eat and drink, and find satisfaction in all their toil—this is the gift of God."

The best daily bread is a dose of happiness to toast
Eat, drink, and be merry for
nourishment and not to boast
There is no greater joy than to do good while you live
The satisfaction that the toiling supplied
the gifts you have to give

Contributed by: Debra Domino

AUGUST 2

Colossians 3:12 "Therefore, as God's chosen
people, holy and dearly loved, clothe
yourselves with compassion, kindness,
humility, gentleness and patience."

The compassion of friendliness opens
the door for friendship
The mutual affection of kindness forms the relationship
The interpersonal connection distinctively yearns
To have the best interest and welfare
of each other's concerns

Contributed by: Debra Domino

AUGUST 3

Genesis 1:29 "And God said, Behold, I have given you every herb bearing seed, which is upon the face of all the earth, and every tree, in the which is the fruit of a tree yielding seed; to you it shall be for meat."

From the seeds in the earth to
blossoms and herbal blooms

The summer's fresh fruit are delicious to consume

Yielding from vines, sprouts, to trees
filled with succulent treats

A harvest to satisfy joyful festivities and great eats

Contributed by: Debra Domino

AUGUST 4

Philippians 1:9-11 "And this is my prayer: that your love may abound more and more in knowledge and depth of insight, [10]so that you may be able to discern what is best and may be pure and blameless for the day of Christ, [11]filled with the fruit of righteousness that comes through Jesus Christ—to the glory and praise of God."

Knowledge and training provide
insight to help build expertise

In-depth experience of techniques
makes advancements increase

Implementations move forward to
enhance system operations

Love abounds with insight to create
new product innovations

Contributed by: Debra Domino

AUGUST 5

Proverbs 31:12-16 [12]"She brings him good, not harm, all the days of her life. [13]She selects wool and flax and works with eager hands. [14]She is like the merchant ships, bringing her food from afar. [15]She gets up while it is still night; she provides food for her family and portions for her female servants. [16]She considers a field and buys it; out of her earnings she plants a vineyard."

The many routes of a working woman drive the success
Moving and doing day and night
pushing through duress
Providing food for her family with eager hands
Always thinking and planning to handle new demands

Contributed by: Debra Domino

AUGUST 6

Ecclesiastes 2:24 "There is nothing better for a man than to eat and drink and tell himself that his labor is good. This also I have seen that it is from the hand of God."

A summer day to quench thirst by
enjoying beverages of the season

Loving life's blessings and the rewards
of labor give the reason

To relax and celebrate today with
a moment of refreshment

Appreciation with gratitude gives
boost to the nourishment

Contributed by: Debra Domino

AUGUST 7

Psalm 27:1 "The LORD is my light and my salvation- whom shall I fear? The LORD is the stronghold of my life- of whom shall I be afraid?"

Like the lighthouse of maritime navigation
The stronghold of the light brings salvation
Deliverance, rescue, recovery, relax - do not fear
The trust and belief that the shining armor is near

Contributed by: Debra Domino

AUGUST 8

Psalm 37:4 "Take delight in the LORD, and he will give you the desires of your heart."

Relax and find happiness in a quiet
moment of self-reflection

Think of your heart's desires and
make a mental projection

What's seen and believed gives
confidence and motivation

The delight in knowing you take the
steps to your own elevation

Contributed by: Debra Domino

AUGUST 9

1 Timothy 3:16 – All scripture [is] given by inspiration of God, and [is] profitable for doctrine, for reproof, for correction, for instruction in righteousness:"

Scriptures are given for instruction and inspiration

The meanings are open to each person's translation

The doctrines give guidance for study and evaluation

The application of what's learned incite revelation

Contributed by: Debra Domino

AUGUST 10

Proverbs 18:9 "He also that is slothful in his
work is brother to him that is a great waster."

The lazy days of summer can feel
like a good time of sloth
Ongoing lethargy is not stylish to wear the lazy cloth
Too much idleness can come with a great cost
Time can be wasted but unproductivity makes for loss

Contributed by: Debra Domino

AUGUST 11

Proverbs 22:6 "Train up a child in the way he should go; even when he is old he will not depart from it."

A special day to bond with your daughters and sons
The joys of life come with having simple family fun
Train up the children and teach them the way to go
The raising instilled will mean more
than you may ever know

Contributed by: Debra Domino

AUGUST 12

Hebrews 10:35 "Therefore do not throw away
your confidence, which has a great reward."

Self-assurance is a great building
block and helper for discovery

It can come with visions and
innovations that help recovery

An idea about something that seems impossible

Could be the resource that finds cures
and makes other things plausible

Contributed by: Debra Domino

AUGUST 13

Mark 10:40 "But to sit at my right hand or at my left is not mine to grant, but it is for those for whom it has been prepared."

The hands anointed by God are helpers
both the left and the right

To use and provide support for many
uses and makes a fist to fight

Thumbs up, high fives, and handshakes
make handling marvelous

Hands to care and build with purpose
makes them also industrious

Contributed by: Debra Domino

AUGUST 14

Job 29:6 "When my path was drenched with cream
and the rock poured out for me streams of olive oil."

Refreshing, cleansing, saturation on
the path of your excursion

Drenched with oils to smooth the way
and awaiting your emersion

Cream rises to the top and can be the face of a rock

Solid and stalwart as a door just waiting for your knock

Contributed by: Debra Domino

AUGUST 15

John 14:1 "Do not let your hearts be troubled.
You believe in God; believe in Me as well."

A day to breathe in and relax your mind

A calm moment of silence helps to unwind

Let not your heart be troubled and distressed

Believe with your heart that all
concerns will be addressed

Contributed by: Debra Domino

AUGUST 16

Psalm 126:2 "Then our mouth was filled with laughter, and our tongue with shouts of joy; then they said among the nations, "The Lord has done great things for them."

A day filled with humor and laughter
can bring joy and ease

The pleasure filled emotion can
make the heart feel pleased

The action comes with lighthearted
thoughts that stimulate

The mind to think happily and let the burdens eradicate

Contributed by: Debra Domino

AUGUST 17

Proverbs 6:6-8 "Go to the ant, thou sluggard;
consider her ways, and be wise: [7]Which having no
guide, overseer, or ruler, [8]Provideth her meat in the
summer, and gathereth her food in the harvest."

This is a day to plan a budget to shop by being thrifty

Like the strategic gathering of the
ant which is quite nifty

Without a guide or overseer the ant carries out the plan

Look for bargains and sales to leave
more bucks in your hand

Contributed by: Debra Domino

Deuteronomy 8:18 "But remember the LORD
your God, for it is he who gives you the ability
to produce wealth, and so confirms his covenant,
which he swore to your ancestors, as it is today."

The ability to produce wealth is already confirmed
It is part of the covenant ready to be affirmed
Sworn into the ancestry to have and to hold
For your passion and legacy to let the story be told

Contributed by: Debra Domino

AUGUST 19

Proverbs 11:25 "The generous soul will be made rich,
And he who waters will also be watered himself."

Generosity is a bountiful act of kindness for the sum of the wh

Humanitarian efforts for one cause can help another cause unfc

The giver helps the receiver, the receiver becomes a giver

It all comes together to make greatness be delivered

Contributed by: Debra Domino

AUGUST 20

John 15:16-17 "You did not choose me, but I
chose you and appointed you so that you might
go and bear fruit—fruit that will last—and so that
whatever you ask in my name the Father will give
you. [17]This is my command: Love each other."

The trees bear different fruit for food to eat
Like that of a lemon that can be bitter and sweet
A mixture of tart and sweet makes a cocktail to aid
In the quenching of thirst making delicious lemonade

Contributed by: Debra Domino

AUGUST 21

Job 12:12 "Is not wisdom found among the aged?
Does not long life bring understanding?"

Aging is like a seasoning that sprinkles
on wisdom and prudence

The spice of wisdom gives farsightedness and assurance

The understanding and observation
that get renewed each day

The providential guidance of the divine pathway

Contributed by: Debra Domino

AUGUST 22

Psalm 91:11 "For he will command his angels concerning you to guard you in all your ways;"

An angel in disguise is seen through kindness
A good friend or companion or any act of the finest
A prayer that's answered in the form of a good deed
A guardian that shows up right in the time of need

Contributed by: Debra Domino

AUGUST 23

Romans 13:8 "Let no debt remain outstanding, except the continuing debt to love one another, for whoever loves others has fulfilled the law."

Fulfillment with the currency of Love comes free

It gives the freedom to set the budget
to whatever you want it to be

Imperfections can be cured and healed from flaw

Giving pure love is a fulfillment of the law

Contributed by: Debra Domino

AUGUST 24

Corinthians 10:17 "For we being many
are one bread, and one body: for we are
all partakers of that one bread."

Each one of us becomes many to make up life's bread
One body comes together with many heads
Give us this day our daily bread
The sustenance of life for all to be fed

Contributed by: Debra Domino

AUGUST 25

Mark 11:25 "But when you are praying, first forgive anyone you are holding a grudge against, so that your Father in heaven will forgive your sins, too."

Making up from break ups makes the heart feel lighter
Settling a grudge can make the day feel brighter
Forgiving is a powerful act that calms and placates
It is freeing to move the barriers that block and stagnate

Contributed by: Debra Domino

AUGUST 26

Ephesians 2:14 "For he himself is our peace, who
has made the two groups one and has destroyed
the barrier, the dividing wall of hostility,"

Equality is a balancer to remove the barriers that divide
Resolving the conflict promotes peace and provides
All parts can accomplish more without the hostility
Reasoning and resolutions with hope and tranquility

Contributed by: Debra Domino

AUGUST 27

Hebrews 7:24 "but because Jesus lives forever,
he has a permanent priesthood."

A day to think about just because

Take a moment to meditate and pause

Just because of a life that lived before

A permanent life can live forever more

Contributed by: Debra Domino

AUGUST 28

Proverbs 4:23-24 "Above all else, guard your heart, for everything you do flows from it. [24]"Keep your mouth free of perversity; keep corrupt talk far from your lips"

A day to spread the spirit of
thoughtfulness and goodwill

Thoughts that flow from the heart
can control how you feel

Perverse words and thoughts can corrupt the mind

The ripple effects of generosity can inspire being kind

Contributed by: Debra Domino

AUGUST 29

James 1:2-3 "Consider it pure joy, my brothers
and sisters, whenever you face trials of many
kinds, [3]because you know that the testing
of your faith produces perseverance."

Trials come and go but survival through
them builds perseverance

It becomes a powerful test of faith
to hold on for deliverance

Making it through a storm is a feat of exultation

Consider it joy and a state of jubilation

Contributed by: Debra Domino

AUGUST 30

Isaiah 61:2 "And I will pray the Father, and he shall
give you another Comforter, that he may abide with
you forever; Isaiah 61:2." NIV "to proclaim the
year of the LORD's favor and the day of vengeance
of our God, to comfort all who mourn,"

Self-care is vital especially during a time of loss
Changes occur with results that affect the cause
May the comfort and favor help you to abide
Your feelings are emotions ready to heal and not hide

Contributed by: Debra Domino

AUGUST 31

Genesis 12:2 "I will make you into a great nation, and I will bless you; I will make your name great, and you will be a blessing."

The word August means distinguished
and impressive with respect

What a great month to show your
self-worth and not neglect

The passion and desires of what you really want see

The matching and making of whatever you choose to be

Contributed by: Debra Domino

SEPTEMBER 1

Psalm 119: 1 "Blessed are those whose way is blameless, who walk in the law of the LORD. Blessed are those whose ways are blameless, who walk according to the law of the LORD. Joyful are people of integrity, who follow the instructions of the LORD. Blessed are those whose way is blameless, who walk in the law of the LORD!"

We need the blessings of always being wrapped in the arms of the Lord, so that we may feel the peace of being protected and loved.

Quoted By: Doris Freeman (Sister Love)

SEPTEMBER 2

Psalms: 9:9 "The LORD is a shelter for the oppressed, a refuge in times of trouble. The LORD is a stronghold for the oppressed, a stronghold in times of trouble."

Let go of the stress and clutter in your life. Distance yourself from toxic people, and cherish the gifts of from kindness and embrace the good will of God, through prayer and faith. Exhale the stress and be more blessed.

Quoted By: Doris Freeman (Sister Love)

SEPTEMBER 3

James 1:2-4 "Count it all joy, my brothers when you meet trials of various kinds, for you know that the testing of faith produces steadfastness. And let steadfastness have its full effect, that you may be perfect and complete, lacking in nothing."

Gratitude makes a positive attitude. Be Grateful for all your blessings, be grateful for your trials. Trials give you the ability to grow.

Quoted By: Doris Freeman (Sister Love)

SEPTEMBER 4

"Matthew 5:16: Let your light so shine before
men, that they may see your good works
and glorify your Father in heaven."

Drink a cup of awesomeness each morning,
let it overflow with peace love and joy. Make
somebody smile today by doing a good deed.

Quoted By: Doris Freeman (Sister Love)

SEPTEMBER 5

Timothy 2:23 "The Lord Jesus Christ be with
your spirit. Grace be with you. Amen."

Open your gifts and explore the challenges
that are ahead of you today.

Quoted By: Doris Freeman (Sister Love)

SEPTEMBER 6

Ezekiel 28:4 "You have acquired riches for yourself, and have acquired gold and silver for your treasuries."

We can climb the mountain to get to great health, wealth and prosperity, and come down on the other side victorious. Just take one step to begin the journey. Carry faith and strength, and God will be beside you.

Quoted By: Doris Freeman (Sister Love)

SEPTEMBER 7

Proverbs 16:11 "A just balance and scales belong to the Lord; All the weights of the bag are His concern."

Life is like the scales of the Zodiac sign for Libras.
Libras are constantly trying to keep balanced.
(Libra is the Zodiac sign for September.)

Quoted By: Doris Freeman (Sister Love)

SEPTEMBER 8

Proverbs 18:2 "A fool takes no pleasure in understanding, but only in expressing his opinion."

People vent just to have an ear to listen.
Your advice is not needed. Only oneself can
make the right choice about their life.

Quoted by: Doris Freeman (Sister Love)

SEPTEMBER 9

Thessalonians 5:16-18 "Rejoice always, pray continually, give thanks in all circumstances; for this is God's will for you in Christ Jesus. I am thankful, right now, Lord Jesus. Help me to remember to be thankful tomorrow when… What's Next?"

Each morning we awake to hear the ticking of our hearts, be thankful to God for allowing us to wake up. The constant beat of the heart is the center of our existence and works jointly with the brain to make the vehicles of our bodies run smoothly.

Quoted by: Doris Freeman (Sister Love)

SEPTEMBER 10

Proverbs 10:12 "Hatred stirs up strife:
but love covers all sins"

Life is full of chaos and strife, that is thrown into our
lives daily. It makes us pray harder and think smarter.

Quoted by: Doris Freeman (Sister Love)

SEPTEMBER 11

Matthew 24:9 "Then they shall deliver you up
to be afflicted, and shall kill you: and ye shall
be hated of all nations for my name's sake."

Today is a very monumental and sacred day. On
this day September 11, 2001, two separate planes
flew into the twin towers of the World Trade center
in New York City. The number of people who
died was 2977, and more than 6000 injuries. This
was an act of hatred and violence. Let us always
remember those who died in vain and in pain.

Hatred and violence continue to storm our
country and the world. We must continue to fight
for what we believe in. Suit up and accept the
challenges. One day we will win the fight.

Quoted by Doris Freeman (Sister Love)

SEPTEMBER 12

Psalm 18:2 "The LORD is my rock, my
fortress, and my deliverer. My God my strength
in whom I will trust, my shield, and the
horn of my salvation, my stronghold."

Be thankful for another day of sunrise. Accept the
blessing of being able to wake up, walk on top of
the ground instead of being under the ground. God
has allowed life for another day. Always walk in the
light, and Jesus is walking with you constantly.

Quoted by Doris Freeman (Sister Love)

SEPTEMBER 13

Mark 11:24 "Therefore I tell you, whatever you ask in prayer, believe that you have received it, and it will be yours."

Pray for what you need. Conceive it, believe it, and receive it. When it seems impossible, believe the possible. It can and will happen.

Quoted by Doris Freeman (Sister Love)

SEPTEMBER 14

Hebrews 11:1 "Now faith is the substance of things hope for, the evidence of things not seen."

Many times, in our life it may look like we have come to the end of the road, then God will whisper, "keep going." Soon you will be able to see the bend at the end. Do not forget to rejoice and praise him.

Quoted by Doris Freeman (Sister Love)

SEPTEMBER 15

John: 14:1 "Let not your heart be troubled;
you believe in God, believe also in me."

When the storm is raging keep holding on. Watch
how you will end up on top of the rainbow.
You may give out, but never give up.

Quoted by Doris Freeman (Sister Love)

SEPTEMBER 16

1 Corinthians 16:14. "Let all that
you do be done with love."

A new day, and a new way to celebrate
and bask in the sunlight of love. Each day
is a new favor with a new flavor.

Quoted by Doris Freeman (Sister Love)

SEPTEMBER 17

Nehemiah 8:10 "Do not grieve, for the joy of the Lord is your strength."

We need strength to keep our joy, and joy to keep our strength. Let us focus on the eye of the sparrow, instead of what is around it. This will bring us the strength we need to grab the joy.

Quoted by Doris Freeman (Sister Love)

SEPTEMBER 18

Hebrew 13:15 "Therefore by him, let us continually
offer sacrifice of praise to God that is, the fruit
of our lips, giving thanks to his name."

Be thankful for any blessings, no
matter how small or large.

Quoted by Doris Freeman (Sister Love)

SEPTEMBER 19

Deuteronomy 8:18 "But remember the Lord
your God, for it is he who gives you the ability
to produce wealth, and so confirms his covenant,
which he swore to your ancestors as it is today."

May he walk with us and talk with us, lead us into
the riches of the mind, heart, soul, and life. May he
pick us up and carry us through the trials, taking
us to safety for health, wealth, and prosperity.

Quoted by Doris Freeman (Sister Love)

SEPTEMBER 20

Psalms 139:13. "For you formed my innard parts, you covered me in my mother's womb."

His creation of me is not perfect, but is perfect for the plans he had/has for me. I with continue to move forward as he leads me.

Quoted by Doris Freeman (Sister Love)

SEPTEMBER 21

Mathew 7:13-14 "Enter by the narrow gate; for wide is the gate, and broad is the way that leads to destruction and there are many who go in by it. 14. Because narrow is the gates, and difficult is the way which leads to life, and there are few who finds it."

Choose the road not taken, and make it a major highway, then turn it into the biggest interstate. It will be your own testament.

Quoted by Doris Freeman (Sister Love)

SEPTEMBER 22

Proverbs 3:6 "In all your ways acknowledge
him, and he shall direct your paths."

God is the master at forgiveness, yet we have those
that keep hatred and darkness in their hearts forever.
Let us release the darkness so that we may see the
brightness of the light so that we may receive joy.

Quoted by Doris Freeman (Sister Love)

Psalms 4:1 "Hear me when I call O God of my righteousness. You have relieved me in my distress, have mercy on me and hear my prayer."

Keep the main line open and flowing through your way. Call him up each day and thank him for the many blessings he has bestowed upon us. Even with the shimmer of darkness and evil, his bright light still shines through. When I get weak, he strengthens me. When I fail, he makes me succeed.

Quoted by Doris Freeman (Sister Love)

SEPTEMBER 24

John 19:4-5 [4]"Jesus also knowing all things would come upon him, went forward and said to them "whom are you seeking?" [5]"They answered him "Jesus of Nazareth. Jesus said, "I am He." "And Judas who had betrayed him also stood with them."

The devil will do a sneak attack when you think things are going well, just to mess up your heart and mind. Then, God surrounds us and sweeps it all away. Thank him for his grace and mercy.

Quoted by Doris Freeman (Sister Love)

SEPTEMBER 25

I John 5:14 "Now this is the confidence we have in Him, that if we ask him anything according to His will, He hears us."

Make sure that ingredients of your past do not make a dry cake. If the cake is blended well, you will love the taste of it. Praying keeps the cake fresh and soft. Enjoy your day.

Quoted by Doris Freeman (Sister Love)

SEPTEMBER 26

Psalms 100:2 "Serve the Lord with gladness, come before his presence with singing".

Difficult times have truly been testing our Faith. Things could be worse, be thankful for the blessings that are bestowed upon us. Making one step at a time, be Thankful for life.

Quoted by Doris Freeman (Sister Love)

SEPTEMBER 27

1 Corinthians 15:58 "Therefore my beloved
brethren, be steadfast, immovable, always
abounding in the work of the Lord, knowing
that your labor is not in vain in the Lord."

His blessings are amazing. He is a maker out of no way.
Life is a hard road to travel, but if we keep driving,
an abundance of blessings will appear. Let's keep our
hands on the wheel and keep our focus on the road.

Quoted by Doris Freeman (Sister Love)

SEPTEMBER 28

1 Corinthians 16:9 "For a great and effective door has opened to me, and there are many adversaries."

He continues to open doors when other doors close. Without his love and protection, we would have nothing. Prayers for continued blessings for us all.

Quoted by Doris Freeman (Sister Love)

SEPTEMBER 29

Matthew 6:28 "So why do you worry about clothing?" "Consider the Lillies of the field; how they grow, they neither toll or spin."

I would like to walk through the lilies of the valley to smell the sweetness of his name, feel the touch of his love, hear the ripple of breath, see the glory that he brings, hear his amazing grace, and taste his power of protection. Blessings today and always.

Quoted by Doris Freeman (Sister Love)

SEPTEMBER 30

Romans 12:2 "And do not be conformed to
this world, but be transformed by the renewing
of your mind, that you may prove what is that
good and acceptable, and perfect with God."

We depend on God backing us daily. Thanking him
for allowing us to wake up this morning, and making
each step to more wisdom, knowledge, and love.

Quoted by Doris Freeman (Sister Love)

OCTOBER 1

Luke 12:7 "And even the very hairs of your head are all numbered. So do not be afraid; you are worth more than many sparrows. Indeed, the very hairs of your head are all numbered."

Your crowning glory is your dome and design
The expression of your style is for you to define
Sprouting from the many follicles and numbered
Adorning pockets of gold so no
need to feel encumbered

Contributed by: Debra Domino

OCTOBER 2

Nahum 2:4 "The chariots storm through the streets, rushing back and forth through the squares. They look like flaming torches; they dart about like lightning."

The technology of the automobile has become essential

The many different kinds range
from modest to influential

The reliability of having a nice
chariot for work and pleasure

Adds meaning to this life and memories to treasure

Contributed by: Debra Domino

OCTOBER 3

Numbers 6:24-26 "The Lord bless you. and keep you; [25]the Lord make his face shine on you. and be gracious to you; [26]the Lord turn his face toward you. and give you peace."

Today is one to celebrate and cultivate you

May blessings shine upon you with the perfect hue

Enjoy and give thanks for every minute of each day

Find your own inner peace to live your life your way

Contributed by: Debra Domino

OCTOBER 4

John 1:11 "He came to that which was his
own, but his own did not receive him."

Being genuine is owning who and for what you stand

Many may receive you and others
may raise a different hand

Staying true to yourself is a powerful virtue

It is you who controls the life you desire to nurture

Contributed by: Debra Domino

OCTOBER 5

Ephesians 4:32 "Be kind and compassionate
to one another, forgiving each other, just
as in Christ God forgave you."

Being nice is a gesture that's attractive

It is a courtesy that can be reactive

Spontaneous compassion can be contagious

It garners respect from others and the return is gracious

Contributed by: Debra Domino

OCTOBER 6

Galatians 6:2 "Carry each other's burdens, and
in this way you will fulfill the law of Christ."

A good coach is one who supports but without demands

A burden can be relieved with a good coach at hand

The sharing of expertise and
instructions for reaching goals

Fulfills the laws of Christian duty
with an empowering role

Contributed by: Debra Domino

OCTOBER 7

Peter 3:4 "Rather, it should be that of your inner
self, the unfading beauty of a gentle and quiet
spirit, which is of great worth in God's sight."

The beauty of life's nature shows all around
The nature of self is where beauty is also found
The seasons replenish nature with beauty parading
A gentle and loving spirit is beauty unfading

Contributed by: Debra Domino

OCTOBER 8

John 15:13 "Greater love has no one than this,
that someone lay down his life for his friends."

Heroes are all around and show up
in many different ways
What a great way to respond to help make another's day
A hero can be a parent, a teacher,
or a role model to admire
Heroes see, believe, and guide in
ways to support and inspire

Contributed by: Debra Domino

OCTOBER 9

Jeremiah 29:13 "You will seek me and find me
when you seek me with all your heart."

Seek and find the discovery of your own place
In that search lies the connection to your personal space
All that you will ever need is granted for your glory
There is no need to settle in another's territory

Contributed by: Debra Domino

Jeremiah 30:17 "But I will restore you to health and heal your wounds,' declares the LORD, 'because you are called an outcast, Zion for whom no one cares."

Mental wellness is important for physical health

The effects of the mind can creep in like a stealth

Emotions can be misunderstood and cause enigmas

Awareness and education are keys to counter the stigma

Contributed by: Debra Domino

OCTOBER 11

Leviticus 19:18 "Do not seek revenge or bear
a grudge against anyone among your people,
but love your neighbor as yourself."

Connections with others can cause emotions to stir
Bullying and other torment become difficult to deter
It can happen so quickly and very easy to persuade
Love your neighbor as yourself and
let the vengeance fade

Contributed by: Debra Domino

OCTOBER 12

Philippians 4:8 "Finally, brothers and sisters, whatever is true, whatever is noble, whatever is right, whatever is pure, whatever is lovely, whatever is admirable—if anything is excellent or praiseworthy—think about such things."

A day for free thought to think about whatever
Doing whatever is right for you is being clever
Thinking of things that are
admirable and commendable
Inspires motivation to do whatever
makes you feel dependable

Contributed by: Debra Domino

OCTOBER 13

Isaiah 60:22 "The least of you will become a thousand, the smallest a mighty nation. I am the LORD; in its time I will do this swiftly." The least of you will become a thousand, the smallest a mighty nation."

Be encouraged and steadfast that
your actions will multiply
Just as the old cliché of how the time will certainly fly
Swiftly it may occur like the blink of an eye
A change can come that makes a
small vision reach the sky

Contributed by: Debra Domino

Nehemiah 8:10 "Nehemiah said, "Go and enjoy choice food and sweet drinks, and send some to those who have nothing prepared. This day is holy to our LORD. Do not grieve, for the joy of the LORD is your strength."

A day to enjoy a choice of something good to eat

It may be a dessert prepared or a special treat

Relish the moment with appreciation and care

Share with others who were unable to prepare

Contributed by: Debra Domino

OCTOBER 15

John 19:11 "Jesus answered, "You would have no power
over me if it were not given to you from above."

Acknowledge the relationship of the
boss and the subordinate

The secondary and primary are like
complimenting coordinates

A team with responsibilities that
work together with goals

Each has the power to make things
happen within their distinct roles

Contributed by: Debra Domino

OCTOBER 16

1 Corinthians 9:24-25 "Do you not know that in a race all the runners run, but only one gets the prize? Run in such a way as to get the prize. [25]Everyone who competes in the games goes into strict training. They do it to get a crown that will not last, but we do it to get a crown that will last forever."

Any sport takes passion and dedication for training

It takes perseverance and practice without waning

Sports are fun to engage and to
celebrate winning the game

Champions arise but the real sport is not about the fame

Contributed by: Debra Domino

OCTOBER 17

Psalm 34:1 "I will extol the LORD at all times;
his praise will always be on my lips."

A message with meaning that is spoken to be heard

Carries much power for the hearers of the word

Speak so that your faith and belief may be edified

A great delivery that will be received and ratified

Contributed by: Debra Domino

OCTOBER 18

Hebrews 12:14 "Make every effort to live in peace
with everyone and to be holy; without holiness
no one will see the Lord. Make every effort
to live in peace with everyone and to be holy;
without holiness no one will see the Lord."

Humbleness and sincerity open the door for compromise

An apology with the intent to forgive satisfies

Efforts to live in peace with everyone gratifies

Continued commitment for reconciliation fortifies

Contributed by: Debra Domino

OCTOBER 19

1 John 5:14 "This is the confidence which we have before Him, that, if we ask anything according to His will, He hears us. And if we know that He hears us in whatever we ask, we know that we have the requests which we have asked from Him."

Confidence takes practice to develop
poise and composure

Asking and believing is acceptance of the disclosure

Having success with the request builds self-assurance

Doing according to the will promotes
the strength for endurance

Contributed by: Debra Domino

Proverbs 3:27 "Do not withhold good from the deserving when it is within your power to act."

Acknowledging the good that one
does is not to withhold

Recognition is a powerful act of letting a story be told

Anything that makes something
better is worthy of praise

The impact of doing a good job
or deed goes a long ways

Contributed by: Debra Domino

OCTOBER 21

1 Peter 5:7 "Casting all your anxieties
on him, because he cares for you."

Worries and concerns can cause much apprehension
The stress from the emotions trigger tension
Get to a quiet place and cast the anxiety away
Know that care is there for you so no need to stray

Contributed by: Debra Domino

OCTOBER 22

Proverbs 10:6-7 "Blessings crown the head of the righteous, but violence overwhelms the mouth of the wicked. The name of the righteous is used in blessings, but the name of the wicked will rot."

Targeted criminalization and brutality are unjust
Prayers for mercy during heinous times are a must
Carrying out actions of suppression
are destined to keep a nation ill
The call for amplified works of the
righteous to help the nation heal

Contributed by: Debra Domino

OCTOBER 23

John 17:21 "That all of them may be one, Father, just as you are in me and I am in you. May they also be in us so that the world may believe that you have sent me."

A common stand of many comes
together for the same goal
In that all of them may be one with
each a designated role
A large number can be many yet
the sum can be one resolve
The rationale has the power to help movements evolve

Contributed by: Debra Domino

1 Corinthians 4:6-7 "Now, brothers and sisters, I have applied these things to myself and Apollos for your benefit, so that you may learn from us the meaning of the saying, "Do not go beyond what is written." Then you will not be puffed up in being a follower of one of us over against the other. [7]For who makes you different from anyone else? What do you have that you did not receive? And if you did receive it, why do you boast as though you did not?"

Reverence and acknowledgement
of another's work is ethical

Showing gratefulness for learning
from a mentor is respectable

Being a follower of a great leader
can inspire and motivate

To strengthen skills for self-leadership
to build and procreate

Contributed by: Debra Domino

OCTOBER 25

James 2:18 "But someone will say, "You have faith;
I have deeds." "Show me your faith without deeds,
and I will show you my faith by my deeds."

Words of faith and deeds come
together with responsible acts
Show and tell is supported by accomplishments and facts
A deed achieved started with the effort to believe
That the endeavor would reap the benefits to receive

Contributed by: Debra Domino

OCTOBER 26

Luke 10:2 "He told them, "The harvest is plentiful,
but the workers are few. Ask the LORD of the harvest,
therefore, to send out workers into his harvest field."

The time of the year to see many pumpkins on display
The pumpkin harvest is plentiful and in decorative array
The pumpkin serves for consumption
and other purposes galore
It grows, serves, and sows for its cause and many more

Contributed by: Debra Domino

Proverbs 24:16 "For a righteous man
may fall seven times And rise again, But
the wicked shall fall by calamity."

The fallen leaves of autumn make mulch to fertilize

To enrich and nourish for new growth to rise

Falling down does not mean fading away to stay

It is to regroup, recoup, and rise up in a better way

Contributed by: Debra Domino

OCTOBER 28

Psalm 90:12 "Teach us to number our days,
that we may gain a heart of wisdom."

As each day rises and sets in the space of time

Let knowledge be gained at a steady incline

Each day has meaning and purpose to discern

Days are numbered but filled with much to learn

Contributed by: Debra Domino

OCTOBER 29

Thessalonians 5:6 "So then, let us not be like others, who are asleep, but let us be awake and sober."

The stillness of the night can insight preparedness

The sound of a noise heard during
slumber shows awareness

Be vigilant with attentiveness to
all things with cognizance

The intention of being awake and
sober is a state of consciousness

Contributed by: Debra Domino

OCTOBER 30

Psalm 145:19 "He fulfills the desires of those who fear him; he hears their cry and saves them."

Fear can be a natural reaction and a sign that you care

It can be frightening not knowing
how things might fare

A humble cry for help to get through
brings the assurance

Blessed is the fulfillment that shows up with insurance

Contributed by: Debra Domino

OCTOBER 31

Ephesians 5:11 "And have no fellowship with the unfruitful works of darkness, but rather reprove them."

Halloween is a celebration that can
be fun with candy and treats

Caution is advised because darkness
can throw tricks to defeat

Darkness and evil prevail in attempts
to shatter life's groove

Be aware of unfruitful works just rebuke and reprove

Contributed by: Debra Domino

NOVEMBER 1

Exodus 32:15-16 "Then Moses turned and went down from the mountain with the two tablets of the testimony in his hand, tablets which were written on both sides; [16]The tablets were the work of God; the writing was the writing of God, engraved on the tablets."

Today is one to capture your time
space with your tablet in hand

Write what you see or feel as your
book is your command

Be the author of your next chapter
and take a moment to release

The memoirs, observations, the
journey of your masterpiece

Contributed by: Debra Domino

NOVEMBER 2

Hebrews 11:1 "Now faith is the assurance of things
hoped for, the conviction of things not seen."

Faith as small as a mustard seed still has hope
The confidence in the possibility makes it easier to cope
The conviction that things not seen will soon manifest
The assurance that everything will work out for the best

Contributed by: Debra Domino

NOVEMBER 3

Corinthians 6:19 "Do you not know that your bodies are temples of the Holy Spirit, who is in you, whom you have received from God? You are not your own."

Your body is a spiritual shrine

A beautiful temple made for a lifetime

A vessel carrying the lives of ancestral formations

A sanctuary that holds the secrets of each creation

Contributed by: Debra Domino

NOVEMBER 4

Psalm 118:13 "I was pushed back and about
to fall, but the LORD helped me."

The push back of life's stress can feel like falling
Lean onto the back of faith and
the words of your calling
The belief that if there is still breath, hope is still alive
The supplication for continuance to rise up and thrive

Contributed by: Debra Domino

NOVEMBER 5

Psalm 37:23 "The LORD makes firm the
steps of the one who delights in him;"

Take the steps in knowing of the delight
With firm conviction that the pathway will be in sight
Make the moves with the passion of Gods will
Revel in the glory that a good outcome will yield

Contributed by: Debra Domino

NOVEMBER 6

Psalm 98:4 "Shout for joy to the LORD, all the earth, burst into jubilant song with music;"

Music is a way to communicate with
the emotions of the soul

The inspiring synthesis of the song
unfolds a story to be told

Inflections, reflections, and articulations to stimulate

The mind, body, and soul infused
with jubilant orchestrates

Contributed by: Debra Domino

NOVEMBER 7

Ecclesiastes 8:6 "For there is a right time
and procedure to every purpose, though a
man's misery weighs heavily upon him"

Make the most of your time to serve your intentions

Procedures require drive for process retentions

Misery can deprive and make balancing out of line

Listen to the commands of your
heart to know the right time

Contributed by: Debra Domino

NOVEMBER 8

Proverbs 31:26 "She openeth her mouth with wisdom; and in her tongue is the law of kindness."

Teachers have such an important
role in the lives of students

A newly born child's parent is the
first instructor of prudence

The parent teacher association is a dual partnership

Two-way communication builds the solid relationship

Contributed by: Debra Domino

NOVEMBER 9

Galatians 5:13 "You, my brothers and sisters, were called
to be free. But do not use your freedom to indulge
the flesh; rather, serve one another humbly in love."

The choice to live a great life is what freedom brings

Serving one another with fairness
and liberty let's freedom ring

The endowment with the grant of
love for humanity to thrive

Is the vision of hope and possibility
that keeps the dream alive

Contributed by: Debra Domino

NOVEMBER 10

1 Corinthians 15:41 "The sun has one kind of splendor, the moon another and the stars another; and star differs from star in splendor."

Astrology, astronomy, and the celestial objects of space
Is the science of the universe and
its magnificence in place
Each star has its own splendor and purpose to shine
The majestic aura and the phenomenal evolution of time

Contributed by: Debra Domino

NOVEMBER 11

Isaiah 41:10 "Fear not, for I am with you;
be not dismayed, for I am your God; I will
strengthen you, I will help you, I will uphold
you with my righteous right hand."

A veteran whether voluntary or by draft enlist

A historical contribution of duty was given to service

Thank you for your diligent courage
to take the active call

Thank you for the commitment and
footsteps to help protect us all

Contributed by: Debra Domino

Titus 3:3 "At one time we too were foolish, disobedient, deceived and enslaved by all kinds of passions and pleasures. We lived in malice and envy, being hated and hating one another."

Like the scarlet leaves of Fall's cycle of reproduction
The opportunity comes to turn a
new leaf for reconstruction
Rebuilding from the sins of malice and deception
Turning to honesty and kindness for sincere affection

Contributed by: Debra Domino

NOVEMBER 13

Proverbs 27:17-18 "As iron sharpens iron,
so one person sharpens another. [18]The one
who guards a fig tree will eat its fruit."

Just as an iron sharpens iron, each
partner polishes the partnership

Working together to help each other
improves the relationship

The collaboration of efforts makes
for strong companionship

The foundations built and guarded
reap the rewards of stewardship

Contributed by: Debra Domino

1 Corinthians 1:4 "I always thank my God for you because of his grace given you in Christ Jesus."

A day to say thanks for the special grace
Days flow with events that take their own pace
Find the time to capture your own personal space
Give gratitude for having a place in life's race

Contributed by: Debra Domino

NOVEMBER 15

Isaiah 58:10-11 "If you spend yourselves in behalf of the hungry and satisfy the needs of the oppressed, then your light will rise in the darkness." The LORD will guide you always; he will satisfy your needs in a sun-scorched land and will strengthen your frame. You will be like a well-watered garden, like a spring whose waters never fail. The LORD will guide you always; he will satisfy your needs in a sun-scorched land and will strengthen your frame.

Philanthropic contributions are
generous causes for goodwill

Satisfying the needs of the oppressed
helps to climb many hills

Darkness becomes outshined by the healing light

Strength is built and frames are restored to stand upright

Contributed by: Debra Domino

NOVEMBER 16

Colossians 3:13-14 "Be tolerant with one another and forgive one another whenever any of you has a complaint against someone else. You must forgive one another just as the Lord has forgiven you. [14]And to all these qualities add love, which binds all things together in perfect unity."

Tolerance with one another takes
commitment and assurance
Finding patience can be like an
exercise of mental endurance
Practicing and focusing on the best
outcomes build fortitude
Forgiveness builds resilience that can
emotionally improve the mood

Contributed by: Debra Domino

NOVEMBER 17

Proverbs 13:7 "One person pretends to
be rich, yet has nothing; another pretends
to be poor, yet has great wealth."

States of rich or poor come down to a mindset

Value stated on any worthiness can carry a high bet

Pretentions of plenty may be done for show and deceit

Sincere virtues from the heart are
riches that will never deplete

Contributed by: Debra Domino

NOVEMBER 18

Colossians 3:23 "Whatever you do, work
at it with all your heart, as working for
the LORD, not for human masters."

A day to let your professional etiquette shine

Services rendered with attentive
quality help the bottom line

Working from the heart infuses love and compassion

Skills, heart, and production bring all around satisfaction

Contributed by: Debra Domino

NOVEMBER 19

1 Peter 2:9 "But you are a chosen people, a royal priesthood, a holy nation, God's special possession, that you may declare the praises of him who called you out of darkness into his wonderful light."

The spirit of excellence and being fair is royal
Devotion and dedication to a cause is loyal
Being chosen to royal priesthood can be accepted by all
Being kindhearted and giving is an answer to the call

Contributed by: Debra Domino

NOVEMBER 20

Proverbs 3:3 "Let love and faithfulness never
leave you; bind them around your neck,
write them on the tablet of your heart."

Setting a good example is an admirable role

A role model leads with respect as a goal

Strong men and women speak with discretion

That the love bound in their heart is the true confession

Contributed by: Debra Domino

NOVEMBER 21

Acts 2:17 "Your sons and daughters will prophesy,
your young men will see visions, your old men
will dream dreams. "'In the last days, God says,
I will pour out my Spirit on all people."

Ambitious children have dreams to manifest
There is the responsibility to help
them achieve their best
Learning begins as soon as a child is born
Achieving after the conceiving is the vow to be sworn

Contributed by: Debra Domino

1 Peter 5:14 "Greet one another with a kiss of
love. Peace to all of you who are in Christ."

A greeting is a way of personal communication
It's an expression to establish an initial relation
Saying hello or just flashing a beautiful smile
A kindred spirit of peace goes a long mile

Contributed by: Debra Domino

NOVEMBER 23

Ecclesiastes 9:9 "Enjoy life with your wife,
whom you love, all the days of this meaningless
life that God has given you under the sun-all
your meaningless days. For this is your lot in life
and in your toilsome labor under the sun."

As the celebration of Thanksgiving arrives to the season

What a great way to relish life with purpose and reason

Enjoy your family and the companionship of marriage

Life can be a beautiful journey rolling
in the gratitude carriage

Contributed by: Debra Domino

NOVEMBER 24

Corinthians 10:31 "Whether therefore ye eat, or drink, or whatsoever ye do, do all to the glory of God."

The delight and aroma of a festive
meal with all the dressings

Become possible because of the bestowing of blessings

What a glorious time to be awarded
a day of thanksgiving

To enjoy a meal together with family
members well and living

Contributed by: Debra Domino

NOVEMBER 25

1 Thessalonians 5:18-19 "Give thanks in all circumstances; for this is God's will for you in Christ Jesus. [19]Do not quench the Spirit."

Psalm 107:1 "Give thanks to the LORD, for
he is good; his love endures forever."

Reflecting on the circumstances you had to endure

The thought process reminds of
how you made it through

Giving thanks in all situations shows
the strength to withstand

By holding on to the spirit of God's unchanging hand

Contributed by: Debra Domino

NOVEMBER 26

Psalm 126:3 "The LORD has done great things for us, and we are filled with joy."

The great things that have been done
represent the heart of Thanksgiving

The miracle that connects one day to
the next supports life and living

The celebration of the breath of life
excites the joyful spirit of giving

The care and love for one another
is what makes life fulfilling

Contributed by: Debra Domino

NOVEMBER 27

1 John 1:9 "If we confess our sins, he is
faithful and just to forgive us our sins, and
to cleanse us from all unrighteousness."

In this season of thanksgiving and feasts
Thankfulness and forgiveness help release
The negative energy of sin, with the focus to renew
To cleanse and restore the morality and virtue

Contributed by: Debra Domino

NOVEMBER 28

Deuteronomy 15:10 "You shall generously give to him, and your heart shall not be grieved when you give to him, because for this thing the Lord your God will bless you in all your work and in all your undertakings."

Thanksgiving is giving thanks for giving
A generous offering is the heart delivering
Lending a hand to help another supplies the need
Blessings multiply in measures that satisfy and succeed

Contributed by: Debra Domino

NOVEMBER 29

Philippians 4:6 "In all your ways acknowledge
him, and he will make straight your paths."
Do not be anxious about anything, but in
every situation, by prayer and petition, with
thanksgiving, present your requests to God.

The pathways may curve with angles unknown
Remain steadfast and ask with prayer to be shown
The direction to steer the crooked path straight
With the petition to be victorious
with the fate that awaits

Contributed by: Debra Domino

NOVEMBER 30

2 Chronicles 15:7 "But as for you, be strong and do not give up, for your work will be rewarded."

Finishing and finalizing goals are tests of persistence
To the strength that's built from
faith and being consistent
Continue the work and progress will ensue
Not giving up rewards the award that's overdue

Contributed by: Debra Domino

DECEMBER 1

Philippians 4:13 "I can do all this through
him who gives me strength."

Today begins the month with thirty
days remaining in the year
Symbolic of the poinsettia flower so be of good cheer
For success and strength empowered
from the months before
Believing that the strength will be there forever more

Contributed by: Debra Domino

DECEMBER 2

Luke 2:52 And Jesus grew in wisdom and
stature, and in favor with God and man."

Education fosters growth in wisdom and stature
The favor in understanding is like a freak of nature
Knowledge gained expands clarity and intelligence
Intellect gained inspires motivation and diligence

Contributed by: Debra Domino

DECEMBER 3

Leviticus 19:14-15 "Do not curse the deaf or put
a stumbling block in front of the blind, but fear
your God. I am the Lord. [15]"Do not pervert justice;
do not show partiality to the poor or favoritism
to the great, but judge your neighbor fairly."

It takes wisdom and courage to see
each situation for its abilities

Malpractice towards others reflects
your inner disabilities

Perversion is corruptness destined for destruction

Fairness is conscious objectivity
necessary for reconstruction

Contributed by: Debra Domino

DECEMBER 4

2 Corinthians 9:8 "And God is able to bless you
abundantly, so that in all things at all times, having all
that you need, you will abound in every good work."

Appreciation day is one to have
gratitude for all blessings

Sometimes it brings the heart to
reflection and confessing

It may be someone who has helped you on the way

It may be an unexpected Godsend that made your day

Contributed by: Debra Domino

DECEMBER 5

John 16:13 "But when he, the Spirit of truth,
comes, he will guide you into all the truth. He will
not speak on his own; he will speak only what he
hears, and he will tell you what is yet to come."

There is an old phrase "the truth will set you free"
It is the guiding voice that speaks for you to see
It directs you for the best outcome to be heard
The voice of reason is the light of the word

Contributed by: Debra Domino

DECEMBER 6

John 14:26 "But the Advocate, the Holy Spirit,
whom the Father will send in my name,
will teach you all things and will remind
you of everything I have said to you."

Learning begins as soon as you exit the womb

The immediate cry for food and care shows aplomb

The new life has assurance that someone is there

The reminder that the spirit lives
and the new life is aware

Contributed by: Debra Domino

DECEMBER 7

Psalm 30:5 "For his anger lasts only a moment, but his favor lasts a lifetime; weeping may stay for the night, but rejoicing comes in the morning."

The violence that causes anger is
war that affects a lifetime

The pain that it brings is unfavorable and unkind

The remembrance of lives that have come and gone

It's the favor that comes in celebration
of the love and bravery shown

Contributed by: Debra Domino

DECEMBER 8

Proverbs 18:15 "The heart of the prudent getteth knowledge; and the ear of the wise seeketh knowledge." "The heart of the discerning acquires knowledge, for the ears of the wise seek it out."

Knowledge fuels the mind for broader perspectives

The seeker acquires knowledge to
further advance electives

The auditory response to the intelligence learned

Gives a distinguished level of
advancement of wisdom discerned

Contributed by: Debra Domino

DECEMBER 9

Luke 2:10 "And the angel said unto them, Fear not: for, behold, I bring you good tidings of great joy, which shall be to all people."

Holidays bring the spirit of joy and communication

A beautiful card with touching words can bring elation

Good tidings of great joy can come
with thoughtful words

Expressions from the heart bring good news to be heard

Contributed by: Debra Domino

DECEMBER 10

Psalm 108:12 "Oh give us help against the adversary,
For deliverance by man is in vain. "Give us aid
against the enemy, for human help is worthless."

The plea for human rights and
fairness may seem unheard
Broken promises and historical repeats defy God's words
The deliverance by man can be tainted with adversity
The call for help from the spirit to
show up with diversity

Contributed by: Debra Domino

DECEMBER 11

Isaiah 52:7 "How beautiful on the mountains are the feet of those who bring good news, who proclaim peace, who bring good tidings, who proclaim salvation, who say to Zion, "Your God reigns!"

The climb to a mountain top
metaphorically means good news

The important land mass of the mountain
provides resources to use

Water, tourism, food, and habitats,
standing tall and majestically

A proclamation for salvation and
peace reigning prophetically

Contributed by: Debra Domino

DECEMBER 12

1 Corinthians 3:7 "So neither the one who
plants nor the one who waters is anything,
but only God, who makes things grow."

The beauty of the plant species and their blooms
Bring cheer and fragrance to uplift from gloom
The array of colorful leaves and festive decorations
The splendor of ornaments with bright illumination

Contributed by: Debra Domino

DECEMBER 13

1 Psalm 150:1-6 [1]"Praise the LORD. Praise God in his sanctuary; praise him in his mighty heavens. [2]Praise him for his acts of power; praise him for his surpassing greatness. [3]Praise him with the sounding of the trumpet, praise him with the harp and lyre, [4]praise him with timbrel and dancing, praise him with the strings and pipe, [5]praise him with the clash of cymbals, praise him with resounding cymbals. [6]Let everything that has breath praise the LORD. Praise the LORD."

Many instruments come together for musical cheer
The sounds of music and chorus are joyous to hear
The season of praise and holiday preparation
The tunes of carols to rejoice in celebration

Contributed by: Debra Domino

DECEMBER 14

Genesis 18:6 "So Abraham hurried into the tent to Sarah. "Quick," he said, "get three seahs of the finest flour and knead it and bake some bread.".".

The kneading, leavening, and baking
of bread is an ancient tradition
The process of making bread rise
makes a great rendition
It delivers food for the table and a compliment for wine
The bread winner is the maker of things great and fine

Contributed by: Debra Domino

DECEMBER 15

Matthew 13:46 "When he found one of great value, he went away and sold everything he had and bought it."

Value is an assessment of worth and significance

Finding a pearl or diamond seems worth the remittance

Yet when one finds a quality that
connects with the heart

The value becomes a treasure to cherish and not part

Contributed by: Debra Domino

DECEMBER 16

Acts 3:19 "Repent, then, and turn to God, so
that your sins may be wiped out, that times
of refreshing may come from the Lord."

Days of reconciliation sometimes
involve personal contemplation

A window view sees outside but a
mirror view sees a replication

An examination of the internal view
may feel like condemnation

Release, repent, and refresh for peace and exoneration

Contributed by: Debra Domino

DECEMBER 17

Psalm 46:1 "God is our refuge and strength,
an ever-present help in trouble."

Modern day help can come in many different ways
Whatever form it shows up gives the opportunity to say
Thanks be to God for blessing me today
The refuge of my strength and companion to stay

Contributed by: Debra Domino

Psalm 46:1 "One is so near to another, that no air can come between them. This shows that it cannot be understood of the skin of the whale, and the hardness and strength of that, which is alike and of a piece; whereas those scales, or be they what they may, though closely joined, yet are distinct."

The season of the year to celebrate
wearing an ugly sweater
Colorful and crazy designs of the garment do not fetter

Worn in style by you but it doesn't restrain

It's an expression of a festive spirit
and personality unchained

Contributed by: Debra Domino

DECEMBER 19

Luke 6:38 "Give, and it will be given to you. A good measure, pressed down, shaken together and running over, will be poured into your lap. For with the measure you use, it will be measured to you."

A season of being openhanded is about giving

The altruistic spirit makes for bountiful living

A good measure pours back into your lap to receive

Gifts for your cheerful giving back to you to believe

Contributed by: Debra Domino

DECEMBER 20

John 4:23 "Yet a time is coming and has now
come when the true worshipers will worship
the Father in the Spirit and in truth, for they
are the kind of worshipers the Father seeks."

Many days have gone but the spirit
is present and profound
Today is here now to feel life's beauty all around
To celebrate each new day to see and touch the truth
The burning light of the spirit is effervescent with youth

Contributed by: Debra Domino

DECEMBER 21

Isaiah 60:1 Arise, shine, for your light has come,
and the glory of the LORD rises upon you."

The first day of the winter solstice has
the shortest period of daylight
What a great time to let your inner light shine bright
The holiday season brings decorative illuminations
Arise and align to shine your own brilliant sensations

Contributed by: Debra Domino

DECEMBER 22

Corinthians 15:58 "Therefore, my dear brothers and sisters, stand firm. Let nothing move you. Always give yourselves fully to the work of the Lord, because you know that your labor in the Lord is not in vain."

Continue to be a master of long-term projections
Family life progressions and stability
are under your protection
Let your work speak for itself with
movements for progress
Let the prophetic powers guide you to conquer success

Contributed by: Debra Domino

DECEMBER 23

Genesis 24:7 "The Lord, the God of heaven, who took me from my father's house and from my native land, who spoke to me and swore to me, 'I will give this land to your offspring'—He will send His angel before you, and you can take a wife for my son from there."

The inherent birth right gives you claim to nativity

Your land of origin to take root
and cultivate the facilities

Your roots were spun with character and ingenuity

To live and prosper through generations of perpetuity

Contributed by: Debra Domino

DECEMBER 24

Matthew 1:23 "The virgin will conceive and give birth to a son, and they will call him Immanuel" (which means "God with us)."

John 1:14 "The Word became flesh and made his dwelling among us. We have seen his glory, the glory of the one and only Son, who came from the Father, full of grace and truth."

This day gives honor and glory to the
story of the immaculate conception

The premise gives meaning to
comprehension and perception

A perfect child is born in flesh with
the spirit of grace to cherish

The gift is to life to continue everlasting and not perish

Contributed by: Debra Domino

DECEMBER 25

Isaiah 9:6-7 — "For to us a child is born, to us a son is given... [6]For to us a child is born, to us a son is given, and the government will be on his shoulders. And he will be called Wonderful Counselor, Mighty God, Everlasting Father, Prince of Peace. [7]Of the greatness of his government and peace there will be no end."

A day of celebration of the birth of
greatness for life and being alive

The prophecy that all may seek the
consciousness to live and thrive

With the internal authority to help
guide the path externally

To live with the light of hope to
shine peacefully eternally

Contributed by: Debra Domino

DECEMBER 26

Ephesians 2:8-9 "For by grace you have been saved through faith; and that not of yourselves, it is the gift of God; not as a result of works, so that no one may boast."

A day of thanks for the gifts received

Not to boast about works or status achieved

The gift of grace awarded the present ceremony

A benefactor of favor granted the testimony

Contributed by: Debra Domino

Ecclesiastes 5:18-19 "This is what I have observed to be good: that it is appropriate for a person to eat, to drink and to find satisfaction in their toilsome labor under the sun during the few days of life God has given them-for this is their lot. [19]Moreover, when God gives someone wealth and possessions, and the ability to enjoy them, to accept their lot and be happy in their toil-this is a gift of God."

Eating, drinking, and being merry
are rewards for the employ
The lot of satisfaction is the allotment given to enjoy
Toiling deserves a time to relish the fruits of labor
Wealth and possessions are great gifts of God's favor

Contributed by: Debra Domino

DECEMBER 28

Proverbs 19:1 "Better is the poor that walketh in his integrity, than he that is perverse in his lips, and is a fool."

Delicious Fruit Cakes are prepared and consumed for holiday meals

The term may be compared to the eccentric with peculiar appeals

The integrity of the spirit may be unconventional but sincere

Unusual with upright character bring strengths to revere

Contributed by: Debra Domino

DECEMBER 29

Ecclesiastes 7:14 "In the day of prosperity be joyful, and in the day of adversity consider: God has made the one as well as the other, so that man may not find out anything that will be after him."

Adversity brings appreciation for the days of sunshine
Be joyful for the blessings that are good and kind
Prosperity brings joy to help balance the pain
The journey comes with climbs to get to the gain

Contributed by: Debra Domino

Hebrews 1:3 "He is the radiance of the glory of God and the exact imprint of his nature, and he upholds the universe by the word of his power. After making purification for sins, he sat down at the right hand of the Majesty on high."

Radiant is the glory of the imprint that
marked each day of the year

The power of the universe upheld by
the word becomes very clear

The nature of the state of being is
so miraculously profound

The purification and renewal uplifts
nature to higher ground

Contributed by: Debra Domino

DECEMBER 31

Ecclesiastes 3:11 "He has made everything beautiful in its time. He has also set eternity in the hearts of men; yet they cannot fathom what God has done from beginning to end."

A year of new beginnings with the
dawn of each new day

The eve of the next beginning has arrived
with a new year on the way

The beauty of each day has been
left for each heart to behold

To comprehend the divine meanings
as new stories unfold

Contributed by: Debra Domino

THE INSPIRATIONS OF FAITH, HOPE, AND LOVE

Imagine the beauty of a vessel forever sailing down a river or shore filled with everything needed to sustain life each day. The goods on the vessel never run out and can be chosen to use as often as needed. That gorgeous vessel filled with goods carrying the virtues of Faith, Hope, and Love is ready and waiting to be called upon to deliver fulfillment.

Faith is the belief that the unseen will manifest and deliver when needed. Hope partners with faith with the optimism that the promise will be granted. Love covers Faith and Hope with the shield of protection covering with loving arms, and with the belief that everything will work out to fulfill the common good and goal.

Going to the vessel to call upon Faith, Hope, and Love can illuminate the pathway for the miracle of the promise to shine bright and clear.

Faith, Hope, and Love - for Doing, Becoming, and Overcoming.

1 Corinthians 13:13 "And now these three remain: faith, hope and love. But the greatest of these is love"

Love and Blessings to All,

Debra Domino

NOTES

368

NOTES

NOTES

ABOUT THE AUTHOR

Debra Domino is the author of books Reflections of Omnipotent Love and Open Your Greatest Gift. The inspiration for the book Inspirations Spoken Day By Day - With Faith Hope and Love occurred by being daily witness to acts of faith, hope, love, and kindness that were being rendered. "Sometimes, the most peaceful sanctuary is the dome of the mind and what is visualized and heard by the ears on each side of the dome", says Author Debra Domino. The Author says that "Inspirational thoughts can be calming for the soul." The Author's vision for the book came during a time of crisis when inspiration was what she needed the most to help sustain during life's raging storms.

Printed in the United States
by Baker & Taylor Publisher Services